HELENSBURGH GOLF CLUB

A celebration of the first 100 years

Researched by JIM STARK
Written by DOUGLAS LOWE

PUBLISHED BY HELENSBURGH GOLF CLUB

The support of The Royal Bank of Scotland in the production of this book is gratefully acknowledged.

Dedication:
To the late Douglas B Lowe and to the future generations of Helensburgh golfers.

© Helensburgh Golf Club, 1993.

All rights reserved.

First published in Great Britain in 1993 by Helensburgh Golf Club, East Abercrombie Street, Helensburgh G84 7SQ.

A catalogue record for this book is available from the British Library.

ISBN 0 9520778 0 9

Designed at ScotRun Publications Ltd, Glasgow, by Crawford Mollison & Greg Murphy.
Typeset in 10/14 Palatino.
Colour/Mono Origination by Hiscan, Inverness.
Printed by Highland Printers, Inverness.

Foreword

By the President, Helensburgh Golf Club.

OUR centenary book "Helensburgh Golf Club: A Celebration of the First Hundred Years" should appeal to all members of the club because it provides interesting evidence of the development of the game of golf in Helensburgh.

The book is a record of the history of the club; it illustrates the evolution and development of the course since 1893, and outlines changes in club house facilities over the years. Throughout the century the club increasingly contributed to the game of golf in Dunbartonshire and beyond, and to the sporting and social life of Helensburgh. Surely Helensburgh Golf Club's main strength, and charm, is that essentially it has been a town club - and must remain so.

I congratulate Douglas Lowe and Jim Stark on this interesting record of the club history; members will wish to thank them for their diligent research and work.

Alan Christianson.
November 1992.

Acknowledgements

WE wish to record our thanks for the assistance given in researching this book in particular to Alex Brownlie, May Dalgleish, Alisoun Halligan and Iain McCulloch, to Sandy Houston for the diagrams illustrating the chapter on course evolution, and to John Cleland and Ian McKenna for the individual hole plans.

Additional research was undertaken by Evan McGregor and Frank Platt in Helensburgh's Templeton Library where staff went out of their way to help, as did The Herald library and picture library, particularly Robert Tweedie.

Valuable contributions have also been made by Alex Parker, Tom Inglis, Brian Anderson, Alan Christianson, John Rees, Ian Forsyth, John Munro, John Ashworth, Bob Ralph, Tom Griffiths, Walter Bryden, Denny Scougall, Bob Ferrier, and Nancy McEwan.

Outside assistance is further acknowledged from Ian Bruce, defence correspondent of The Herald for the story of HMS Hood, David Joy of St Andrews for the photograph of Tom Morris, Royal Dornoch Golf Club for background information on Ben Murray, Jack Robertson of the Evening Times for details of Helensburgh's performances in the Evening Times Foursomes, Marjorie Mackie for the photograph of James Braid of whom she is a granddaughter, and Iain Burns of the Scottish Region of the PGA for tournament scores.

Finally, thanks to the juniors for suffering the inconvenience of loss of their room which was taken over for a month during the final stages of compiling the book.

Contents

Chapter 1

Build up to the club's formation   3
From smugglers on the shore to bandits on the hill

Chapter 2

Evolution of the course   9
Foaming billows or precipitous putting proclivities

Chapter 3

The two clubhouses   21
The nineteenth: Never without its loopholes

Chapter 4

The professionals   31
Masters of all trades

Chapter 5

The amateurs   38
The Quarry: Gateway to the world

Chapter 6

Pro tournaments and exhibition matches   53
Wheedling birdies - and birds out of trees

Chapter 7

The officials   58
A higher authority than God, the R & A ... and on a par with Royalty

Chapter 8

Trophies and winners   69
Ben Murray: Biggest hit of the major winners

Chapter 9

Course guides   94
Delights galore for rabbits and tigers alike

CHAPTER 1

Build up to the club's formation

FROM SMUGGLERS ON THE SHORE TO BANDITS ON THE HILL

THE founding of Helensburgh Golf Club on Monday, August 14, 1893, was not before time and several abortive attempts previously had been made. As a leading article in the Helensburgh and Gareloch Times the previous Wednesday had noted: "There are few towns now of any importance but can boast of a golf course . . . The want of such a place of recreation has been felt to be a great hindrance to the prosperity of the town, not only as a health resort, but as a place of residence . . ."

The earliest documentation of golf was at St Andrews in 1552, but there was never any chance of Helensburgh ever getting in on the act as early as that. In those days the land which forms our course was undeveloped and part of the Earldom of Lennox, whose family mansion was at Faslane. At the end of the 18th century the area came into the hands of the Lairds of Luss, the Colquhouns, from whom the club was to buy the course in 1978.

Not until 1802 did the town come into being officially. Sir James Colquhoun had wanted to give his wife, Lady Helen Sutherland, a special birthday present. A diamond necklace? A yacht? No, nothing so common. Instead, Sir James named Helensburgh after her in her honour, but not exclusively so. The town coat of arms is a combination of the crests of the two families, the Colquhouns and the Sutherlands. In that year Helensburgh was created a Burgh of Barony by Royal Charter "in view of encouraging industry and promoting manufacturers."

Even then it was only a small community, comprised largely of weavers, coopers, herring curers and fishermen. There were also illicit distillers and smugglers - definitely a case nowadays of the smugglers on the shore having been replaced by bandits on the hill.

Glasgow merchants could reach Helensburgh reliably in the summer only by wagon, the fly-boats from Broomielaw being notoriously unpredictable. It was not uncommon for the boats to be grounded on sandbanks or becalmed for hours while the Highland crewmen left passengers on board as they nipped ashore to the nearest public house to refresh themselves for several hours while waiting for the tide to come in or the wind to pick up.

If golf had been played in Helensburgh then, one can imagine the rich variety of excuses for failing to arrive on the first tee at the appointed time.

With the arrival of Henry Bell's Comet in 1811, steam navigation was to change the picture, though it was 1830 before a stone dyke was built into the Clyde far enough for passengers to be allowed to land dry-footed. A golf course must have been a low priority, if indeed one at all, but the growing status of the town was soon to demand it.

The construction of the pier and then the arrival of the railway in 1857 opened up Helensburgh. The population grew from 2,895 in 1851 to 4,769 in 1861 and to 6,231 in 1871, by which time mansions comparable with the best country seats were being erected by wealthy Glasgow merchants in the two-acre squares bounded by the distinctive grid-iron street layout, and the town was earning a reputation as Garden Town of the Firth of Clyde.

As a writer of the time commented: "In the summer mornings the atmosphere is at times so laden with sweet perfumes, arising like incense, that you almost realise what dwelling in a land of spices means."

The prosperity of the town insisted on a golf course and so it was to be. When we say it was not before time, in the context of the development of Helensburgh it was perhaps only 15 or 20 years later than it might have been which is not excessive given the problems associated with finding suitable ground.

It is the kind of timescale we are in the midst of on our centenary, with the attempt to win planning permission to sell the historic lower portion of the course for housing and raise the funds necessary for a new clubhouse and to develop land to the north to a total of 27 holes.

Many of the Scottish clubs 100 years or more old have been uprooted on one or more occasions and some have not lasted the pace including many of our neighbours. At one time or another there have been golf courses at Shandon, Garelochhead, Tarbet, Kilcreggan and Finnart. Of those which remain Dumbarton (1888) beat us to it by five years, but we were two years before Cardross and we look forward to welcoming a new neighbour in the Loch Lomond Golf Club at Rossdhu where the course is due to open in our centenary year.

It is a tribute to the care taken by the founders of Helensburgh Golf Club in finding the right spot that the nine holes played at Helensburgh 100 years ago form the basis of the 18-hole course we play today, thus giving complete continuity in one place.

In the August 9, 1893, edition of the Helensburgh and Gareloch Times a public notice, reproduced right, appeared on the front page and inside, the leading article was devoted to the subject. It read:

"The ancient and royal game of golf has of late years been increasing in popularity, and there are few towns now of any importance but can boast of a golf course. Unlike many pastimes, the game appeals to all classes and to both sexes, and, like curling and cricket, it is a great leveller of class distinctions.

The want of such a place of recreation has been felt to be a great hindrance to the prosperity of the town, not only as a health resort but as a place of residence, and time and again efforts have been made to arrange for a course, but, unhappily, these have proved futile.

It is with pleasure now, however, we learn that through the energy and discretion of two public spirited citizens we are within measurable distance of attaining the object in view. Satisfactory arrangements have been made with the tenant farmer, and the trustees and factor on the Luss Estates are giving the scheme every support.

The ground selected lies to the right and left of the old Luss Road, and is admirably adapted for the purpose. It commands a magnificent view of the Clyde, and golfers will enjoy the advantage of the strong mountain air.

The success of the enterprise now rests with the public, and it is to be hoped that it will meet with the liberal encouragement it deserves.

The authorities might, from the common good, contribute towards such an undertaking, and the money would certainly be well spent.

The responsibility, however, rests chiefly with individual householders, and it is for them to turn out on Monday evening to the public meeting, and by a united effort carry the scheme to a successful conclusion."

Despite the counter attractions, on or around the

The public meeting to form the club may not have been the biggest box office hit of the week, but this notice in the Helensburgh and Gareloch Times of August 9, 1893, did the trick.

same time, of an American magician, a performing musical elephant, and a female Scottish singer and comedienne, the townspeople of Helensburgh did what they were urged.

The following week the local paper reported; "A golf club for Helensburgh can now be accepted as an accomplished fact. The public meeting on Monday was large and representative and the enthusiasm augured well for the success of the movement."

William Lunan and Gordon Gemmill "the two public spirited citizens" can be credited with having undertaken the preliminary work in identifying the land on which our course lies, and negotiating access.

At the inaugural meeting in the Court Room of the Municipal Buildings there was reported to be a large attendance, and the first act by Gemmill, who opened the meeting, was to call ex-Provost Alexander Breingan to the chair. Breingan expressed the hope that the meeting would result in steps being taken to form a golf course. Lunan, in turn, suggested that Breingan should be the first club captain because of his enthusiasm for sport, and also because of his track record in bringing to a successful conclusion all things he took up. This was greeted with applause.

Alexander Breingan: the medal the first club captain donated is the oldest in the club's possession.
Picture by John Stuart, reproduced from The Story of Helensburgh.

The stumbling block until this time had been that the Colquhoun Trustees would not sanction the terms of agreement with Mr McAuslane, the tenant of Kirkmichael Farm, but diplomatic manoeuvring had overcome the problems and McAuslane had offered 40 acres of the high parks east and west of the Old Luss Road at an annual rent of 35/- (£1.75p) per acre, the farmer to retain the whole grazing. The lease was to run until 1897.

The Colquhoun Trustees agreed that after 1897 the club could have a new 10-year lease at a rent of 30/- (£1.50) an acre, the club to have grazing rights.

There had been talk of forming a golf course by the Glenan Burn, but Lunan had considered the land there was not sufficiently extensive and that Kirkmichael Farm was the best they could get close to the town.

The estimated costs of the venture make interesting reading, and Lunan reckoned on £380 made up of: Nine putting greens at £15 each, total £135; preparing ground £60 or £70; tools, grass-cutters Etc. £25; clubhouse £150.

The annual running costs would be £160: rent £70 (after expiry of the initial lease this would be £60, reduced considerably by grazing); greenkeeper £65; extras £25.

If these figures seem to us to be outrageously low, they were not so to the pioneers who succeeded within a few weeks of lowering the cost of building the course, though the price of the clubhouse was to be slightly more, Lunan later disclosing that he had obtained a plan of a corrugated iron house which could be erected for less than £200.

To meet costs Lunan supposed a membership of 125 paying 21/- (£1.05p) and 75 juniors and ladies paying half that amount. (Students of arithmetic will note that the subs have since risen by a factor of some 300). This would bring in a total of £170, and he had no doubts a membership of that size could be achieved.

Lunan said the ground had looked all right to some, but he would not go into it without professional advice, and suggested Old Tom Morris, of St Andrews, was asked for his opinion on whether it would make a good golf course.

The proposals were carried unanimously and details were to be worked out by a committee comprising W H Kidston, W Snell Anderson, Alexander Breingan, F G Gemmill, W Lunan, J Spence and J Murray.

It was agreed that the ground be put in order "with the least possible delay and at the least possible cost," and the speed at which events moved from this point is breathtaking. Old Tom Morris visited the proposed site of the course nine days later on August 23, and prepared a report, which sadly has gone missing from the club.

In this, according to a report in the Helensburgh and Gareloch Times, Morris said he had inspected the upper and lower fields of Kirkmichael Farm and considered the two higher fields would make a splendid course when cleaned and the putting greens put in order. The hazards, he thought, were exceptionally fine for an inland course.

Of concern at this time was the location nearby of an army shooting range, but Morris did not foresee any danger from this to golfers.

He considered the holes as suggested were excellently placed, and would not advise on an 18-hole course, feeling that nine holes were ample for the present requirements.

Accompanying Morris over the site were members of the embryonic committee along with Mr Wilson, factor of Luss Estates, and Mr Craig, local agent of the Colquhoun Trustees. The prospect of an 18-hole course was still very much in their mind and Wilson indicated a willingness to talk to the committee whenever the need arose, as was to happen within 12 years.

At the club's next meeting on Tuesday, August 29, the suggestion was made that money for the clubhouse be raised by £5 debentures, which was agreed nine days later, though the sum raised was not to exceed £300 and erection of the clubhouse was to be delayed until work on the course was finished.

At this point, just 24 days after the inaugural meeting, the membership had reached 120. Lunan's original estimate of 125 members plus 75 ladies and juniors was raised to 200 and 100 respectively.

The office bearers were appointed formally: Honorary president, Sir James Colquhoun; president, Richard Kidston; vice-president, Provost Mitchell; captain, Alexander Breingan; secretaries, William Lunan and J M Murray; treasurer, Adrian Kidston; committee, F G Gemmill, John W Spence, W H Kidston, W Snell Anderson, A B Law, and John G Harvey.

If one of these names rings a bell beyond the confines of the golf club or the town, then full marks. He is Andrew Bonar Law, who went on to become Prime Minister in 1923.

On October 7 - 54 days after the first meeting - some enthusiasts were reported to have played the course which was now due for completion by the end of the month at the latest, and the maximum membership had almost been reached.

We can imagine that this unofficial play continued unabated, weather permitting, throughout the winter and following spring right up to the official opening of the course on May 5, 1894. This may be deduced from the remarks of ex-Provost John Mitchell, who, in his opening address, pointed out that the course had been cutting up, and stressed the need for turf to be replaced every time this happened.

Reminders to replace divots have been made at regular intervals since, and we might also imagine that the problem of plug marks on the greens was not so pronounced in those days otherwise this would have been mentioned at the opening as well.

Let that be a warning, and beware the ghost of ex-Provost Mitchell if you ever forget.

A membership of 270 had been reached comprising 170 seniors, 30 below the set maximum, and 100 ladies and juniors.

The opening took place on a rainy day, which will not surprise the present day reader, but a large attendance was reported. Ex-Provost Mitchell referred to an epidemic of golf fever sweeping the country which had now reached Helensburgh, and that his only disappointment was that the course did not extend to 18 holes.

John Mitchell: the vice-president delivered the first reminder to replace divots.
Picture by John Stuart, reproduced from The Story of Helensburgh.

He introduced Breingan, asking if, for the last half century, there had been any improvement to the town which he had neither done himself nor assisted in, and presented to Mrs Breingan an inscribed cleek with which she was to strike the opening shot. Under the circumstances she would have been excused for a duff, but we are led to believe it was a good one. It was reported that she "cleverly drove off the ball amid the cheers of the spectators."

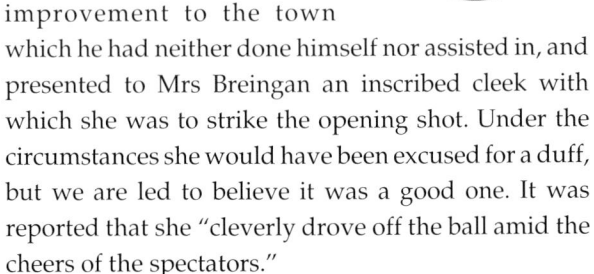

This being on a Saturday, and undoubtedly outwith the permitted hours of play, can be taken as the first infringement of the rules by a lady member, but sanctioned by the captain as is only right and proper.

Captain Breingan also addressed the gathering, congratulating the community on their efforts and revealing that he had taken up the game only the previous year, but assuring everyone that no-one took a deeper interest in the club than he did.

It was at this opening ceremony that he intimated

The pioneers: A group of founder members of Helensburgh Golf club dressed in their Sunday best. Note that nine of the 12 sport beards and that the club mascot in those days was a dog. Alexander Breingan is sixth from the left and John Mitchell third from the right.
Picture provided by Miss Stanton.

he would be donating a gold medal to be competed for by members of the club. The Breingan Medal is the one we play for today and historically is the most significant prize in the club's possession. Mrs Breingan also indicated she would donate a prize for the ladies.

There followed a match between a captain's and vice-president's select team, a tradition which, with a few exceptions, has also survived 100 years, as that is the match which still customarily marks the start of the season, albeit nowadays captain versus vice-captain, the latter office being created in 1947.

In those days the format of team competition was to tally the number of holes up in each match. It was not sufficient just to win, but to do so as handsomely as possible. The result was a win for the captain's side by 13 to 11, the captain himself securing victory by one hole over the vice-president. The details were:

CAPTAIN		VICE-PRESIDENT	
Tulloch	4	Lawson	0
Breingan	1	Mitchell	0
Law	0	Anderson	2
Dingwall	1	F P Smith	0
Todd	2	Webster	0
W Smith	0	Robley	0
Drennan	0	McKim	2
L H Smith	0	Sewell	4
Martin	0	Forrester	3
Malcolm	1	Ormond	0
Arbuthnott	4	Wilson	0
Spence	0	Lunan	0
	13		11

The competitive history of Helensburgh Golf Club had begun.

OLD TOM MORRIS

"Mair saun and nae Sunday play"

Old Tom Morris: three years after visiting Helensburgh he played in his last Open Championship at the age of 75.
Picture courtesy of David Joy, St Andrews.

Tom Morris (1821 - 1908), who at the age of 72 approved the original nine holes at Helensburgh Golf Club, became known as Old Tom in 1851 on the birth of Tom, the eldest of his three sons.

Apart from Helensburgh he had a hand in laying out Lahinch, Westward Ho, Muirfield and Royal County Down among many others. He was one of the pioneers of golf course architecture, though his methods nowadays are regarded as simplistic.

A highly accomplished player Old Tom may have been, but his son was considered far more talented and went on to become one of the all-time great golfers before his tragic death at the age of 24.

Old Tom, a polite and genial man, began his career in his native St Andrews as an apprentice golf ball maker employed by Allan Robertson, the first professional golfer in the game.

At the age of 30 Old Tom headed west for Glasgow and Prestwick after a dispute with Robertson, who resisted the introduction of gutta percha balls because his business was based on the production of the old featheries.

Old Tom, however, saw a future for the cheaper and more durable guttie and went his own way though he never lost respect for Robertson as a player, once describing him as *"the cunningest bit body o' a player that ever handled club, cleek or putter."*

Robertson died in 1858 and was never able to compete in an Open, though there is a view that what is now the world's foremost championship was introduced to establish who was the best player now that he was gone.

In 1860 Old Tom was runner-up to Willie Park at Prestwick in the first Open Championship, but won thereafter in 1861, 1862, 1864 and 1867. He played in every Open from 1860 to 1896 and his final appearance was at the age of 75.

Old Tom returned to St Andrews in 1864 to become the town's golf professional and greenkeeper (his duties almost solely the latter), a base from which he travelled widely in Scotland advising on new courses during the boom time of the late nineteenth century. His fees were £1 a day plus travelling expenses.

He had two strict rules on course maintenance. The first was *"mair saun"*, his belief being that sand was the basis of good turf. This dictum appears to be timeless because Ronnie Myles, on his arrival from Erskine as course manager at Helensburgh, made his first assessment of the greens as needing more sand. The second dictum, *"Nae Sunday play - the course needs a rest even if the gowfers don't"*, was to be observed for more than thirty years.

As a measure of the esteem in which he was held, Old Tom, was the first to be appointed honorary professional of the Royal and Ancient when he retired in 1904 at the age of 83 and the eighteenth green was named the Tom Morris Green in his memory.

Young Tom has been regarded by some historians as the finest natural talent golf has produced. He won his first Open at Prestwick in 1868 aged 17 and took the title again the following two years to win the Championship Belt outright.

There was no Open the following year, but in 1872 his was the first name to be engraved on the present silver claret jug.

Ill health restricted success thereafter to a second place in the next three years, and after his wife died during childbirth in September, 1875, Young Tom was never the same again. He was found dead in his bed on Christmas morning the same year. An autopsy revealed a burst blood vessel in his right lung, but others refused to believe the cause was anything other than a broken heart. *"If that was true I wouldn't be here either,"* Old Tom is quoted as having said.

Old Tom must have gone about his business thereafter with a heavy heart. Father and son are now beyond living memory, but the name is truly immortal and one with which Helensburgh Golf Club can be proud to be associated.

CHAPTER 2

Evolution of the course

FOAMING BILLOWS OR PRECIPITOUS PUTTING PROCLIVITIES

THE continuity of the club over its history is such that we can identify with the original nine holes approved by Old Tom Morris. All are in play today in one form or another, some backwards or sideways, with the exception of the ninth, which crossed the Old Luss Road, and was later to be the 17th before being abandoned. However, various recent versions of winter greens and course have certainly used most of the original to the full.

Features which have since been removed are the dry stane dyke which, if it remained, would now be in front of the present first green and eleventh tee, a fence across the now 13th, 14th, and 15th, and a preponderance of whins, many of which have now been cleared.

The following diagrams showing how the course has changed have been drawn up from old handbooks by Sandy Houston, the one below being the original nine-hole layout.

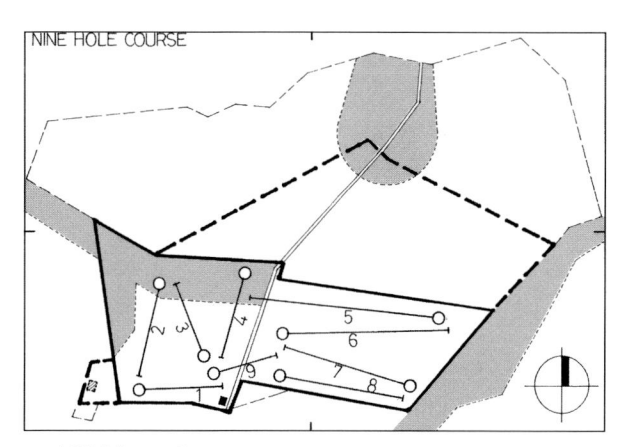

... 1894 layout ..

The course was described in the Glasgow Evening Times on the Thursday prior to the Saturday opening thus:

"After considerable negotiations, the Helensburgh golfers were successful in leasing last autumn several fields adjoining the Old Luss Road for the purpose of being converted into a golf course.

During the winter and spring months workmen have been diligently getting the ground into order, and already many members have had a game over the links.

There are numerous hazards, and altogether the course will be an interesting addition to the numerous attractions of this Madeira of the North.

The first hole (229 yards) is comparatively easy, but a topped ball will be caught in the whins. Four will be good play for this hole.

The second (230 yards) is a most sporting one. It is placed behind a dyke and is surrounded by trees. Correct play should ensure another four.

The tee for the third hole (230 yards) is also among the trees, and a sliced shot will be caught by them, and the dyke is in wait for the topped ball. On each side of the hole is a clump of whins, so that careful approaching will be necessary. The player should get home with four strokes here.

There are more whins to cross on the way to the fourth hole (210 yards), which is beautifully situated at the bottom of an old quarry. There is rough ground in front of the quarry, and, no doubt, many a bad shot will be trapped in it.

In going to the fifth hole (380 yards), the Old Luss Road has to be crossed with the drive. Topped balls will be punished here. A foozled approach shot will come to grief in the dry ditch which guards the hole, which is the longest on the course. Five may be called par play.

The ditch has again to be crossed in going to the sixth (350 yards). There are whins on the left, just lying in wait for a pulled ball. A five here will probably satisfy most golfers.

Whins and the ditch are also the hazards at the next

two holes (350 and 310 yards), which should be negotiated in five and four strokes respectively.

The home hole (110 yards) is reached by a diagonal iron shot across the Luss Road."

The now abandoned 9th green which became the 17th as it was pictured here in May, 1920, and the tee from which it was played. Pencil bags and the wearing of jackets for play was the order of the day.

The topped shot, to which many references are made in this article, was one of the great bugbears of golfers in the latter part of the 19th century.

Looking at the scores posted around the time, often well over 100 for 18 holes, it might be tempting to conclude that our golfing ancestors were less than competent. That, however, would be to misunderstand the nature of of the equipment and state of the course in the early days. The kind of calamity brought on by the topped shot illustrates that the game is now very much different from what is was.

For a start, gutta percha balls were the ones in use until 1902, when the Haskell ball or "Bounding Billy", the direct ancestor of the modern ball, was invented. The gutties were also struck by clubs with shafts made of hickory or ash requiring a much different swing from today. No lesser a person than Jack Nicklaus in his prime discovered this when he tried out such equipment on the Old Course at St Andrews. He succeeded only in duffing the ball a few yards every time.

The guttie, made from the sap of gum trees, made a dull sound when struck, and when topped hardly went anywhere unlike the modern rubber cored or solid ball which can be scudded 200 yards and more in summer conditions. With wooden shafts, moreover, there was the problem of torque which tended to leave the clubface open unless the hands were "thrown" at the ball just before impact.

Steel and carbon shafts have eliminated this problem with the result that the role of the hands in the golf swing today is more passive and greater use is made of the back and leg muscles.

With that background, it is difficult to regard with anything but awe and admiration the score posted on June 22, 1896, by the club professional Tom Turnbull, of 75 - 38 in the first round and 37 on the second - lowering the course record by five shots. On August 13, 1910, over the then 18-hole course and presumably with the new rubber-cored ball, he scored 67 - 31 out and 36 home.

The greens, too, were not the smooth, velvety sort which we expect today and complain about when they are not in that condition. The first major row in the club, surprise, surprise, concerned the greens, and we can gauge some idea of what they were like from an acrimonious exchange of letters in the Helensburgh and Gareloch Times just over a year after the course was opened.

It began with an anonymous poem on March 13, 1895:

OUR GOLF CLUB

We have a goodish golfing course,
Right up the Luss Road hill;
Small matter that the players there
To climb must have a will.

We have a house of shelter too,
Where keep we clubs and clothes
What matter then if on the links
It rains, or snows, or blows?

We have some fairish teeing grounds,
Where one can steady stand;
What does it matter then if some
Have slopes superbly grand.

We have a putting green or two,
Whereon the ball can run;
What signifies if on the rest
No putting can be done?

We have a large directorate,
Composed of active men;
What matter it, if like the gods,
They nod, sir, now and then.

We have a secretary bold,
Indeed a man of mettle;
Small matter that he fails to tell
Accounts are still to settle.

We play a medal round or two,
It helps the hand and eye;
What matter if the scoring cards
Long in the box should lie?

We have a book of handicaps,
Where hopes and fears are centred;
Small matter though for four long months
Naught has therein been entered.

We hold a meeting once a year,
We hear the chairman's voice;
What matter though he praises all?
It makes their hearts rejoice.

And all the men elect again,
They promise to improve;
Small matter if they find it stiff
To quit the grand old groove.

So let us sing, long live the king,
The club, and every member;
And let us live, in peace and love,
Until, well, next December.

This elicited support from a member under the nom-de-guerre Silvertown the following week:

Sir, - I would like to join issue with the writer of the lines of "Our Golf Club" when he says:

"What matter it if on the rest, no putting can be done?"

Now, I say it matters a great deal that, after the expiry of some fifteen months from the time of the opening of the links for play, we can point to but one proper putting green presently available. The committee, in their wisdom, have gone in for a penny-wise, pound foolish policy, instead of tackling the matter at once in a go-ahead and business-like way. Time and money have been frittered away with the result up to the present we have never had the opportunity given us of tasting the delights derivable from putting on a good and true surface.

Can nothing be done to rouse the committee from their present deplorable lethargy?

If, as it would appear, they will not listen to rhyme, is it too much to expect that, in the fulness of time, they may be persuaded to let reason have sway? The fact of the matter seems to be that whilst, as a general rule, a committee exists for the benefit of a club, it would appear that, in our case, a club exists simply for the benefit of a committee, and, until this state of affairs is either ended or mended, any hope for improvement in our putting greens, or, indeed, in anything else connected with our course, may, with perfect propriety, be left till the advent of that most momentous circumstance, the Greek Kalends.

I am &c., Silvertown.

Then came a poetic response, anonymous again, in defence of the club:

OUR GOLF CLUB: A RETURN MATCH

Who says our links are on a hill?
That climbing thereward makes one ill?
The club to pay the doctor's bill.
Small matter.

Who says our house keeps clubs and clothes,
From summer's rain from winter snows?
A place, in fact, to toast one's toes -
And chatter.

Who thinks we have no proper tee
For afternoons? For driving free?
That this is not what ought to be.
No matter.

Who speaks about a putting green?
Perhaps a putter ne'er has seen,
May on a link have never been.
What matter.

Who blames our large directorate,
For rushing blindly to their fate,
By nods the gods might emulate?
Sad matter.

Who says our secretary bold,
Does everything but what he's told?
Such men are worth their weight in gold.
Great matter.

Who fancies every handicap,
Should be like bitter beer - on tap?
Thinks scoring cards are used for nap.
Pure patter.

Who deems the worthy in the chair,
Was far too friendly to be fair?
Much better to have pulled their hair,
Than flatter.

Who thinks committee can't improve,
Themselves from out the same old groove?
Would all the men, in fact, remove.
Mere clatter.

And so the lines to end to bring,
Suggests that all who can should sing -
Long life to our prospective king.
Then scatter.

Further defence came from William Lunan, one of the founding members, who felt the need to justify the integrity of the committee, and on the dominant subject of the greens quoted from an article in the Edinburgh Dispatch about the new course at St Andrews: ". . . the home green, like the majority of the others, is a beautiful broad expanse of turf, not dead level, as some people's idea of a green is, but with ridges and saucers and dips, which makes putting what it really ought to be."

Lunan added: "This new course at St Andrews, as every golfer knows, was laid off by Old Tom Morris, and it goes without saying that no one knows better the requirements of a first class green."

This explanation was anything but accepted. Silvertown responded that he had no objection and quite the reverse to greens "rolling in foaming billows", but he added: "To putt on a precipice as we require to do most assuredly on Number 1, and to a more or less extent on 3, 6, and 7, is, to say the least of it, most distinctly objectionable.

"If the committee believed in the suggestion of Mr Morris as to having the greens in their pristine state plus a little rolling, cutting and top dressing, why were Numbers 1 and 3 returfed without being levelled, incurring additional expense, and at the same time aggravating thereby their previous precipitous putting proclivities."

Other correspondence continued until the editor, probably not before time, called a halt. The issue of the greens, is a controversial one which has persisted on and off throughout the club's history though not since in such a heated and public manner.

As time passed, the situation and the magnificently described precipitous putting proclivities must have improved, though any player today who has tackled a downhill putt at the 3rd or 9th in dry, summer conditions might consider that they have not disappeared entirely.

The improvements are likely to have had much to do with the arrival of E T (Tom) Turnbull as professional in 1895. The initials E T would have a different connotation had he been active in the present era, but there was nothing extra-terrestrial about the man. He was very much down to earth and his additional duties included greenkeeper and general factotum.

Certainly, Dumbartonshire Golf Union, founded in 1896, played the first Wylie Trophy at Helensburgh on October 16, 1897, when, incidentally, Dumbarton won both team and individual prizes - in the days long before the arrival of Charlie Green.

The layout in any case was to last only seven years before it was first altered for practical reasons. By 1900 it was resolved to relocate the original wooden clubhouse close to the West Highland Railway line, thereby allowing easier access to and from the town. There is no record of the modified layout, but one new hole was constructed, and other compensating changes made.

From these early days the only surviving green locations are the first (originally the second) and twelfth (originally the fourth). The twelfth, of course, has recently been reconstructed, but apart from modern bunkers the present first green appears to have survived unscathed, although it did have that dry stane dyke,

Early pictures of the two greens which survive from the original course, the first (below) and the 12th. The first, however, is the only original surface left as the one at the 12th has recently been raised.

which survived for many years, guarding the front.

It is evident that the original venture was, despite its teething troubles, a success, and the demand for golf facilities was increasing. As a result the course was extended to 18 holes by 1905.

The architecture was carried out by Harry S Paul, whose residence in Helensburgh was The White House, and why not if we were to have a member with an address of 10 Downing Street. It would have been apt if he was the club president, but he was referred to in a later article in the Helensburgh and Gareloch Times as Convener. We might presume he was the Greens Convener. The actual laying out of the course was carried out by Turnbull himself, who was experienced in such matters having had a hand in the construction of the Cowal and Newtonmore courses, the latter sharing Helensburgh's centenary.

Again there is no record of the layout at that time, but from a handbook published in 1912 we have a fair approximation.

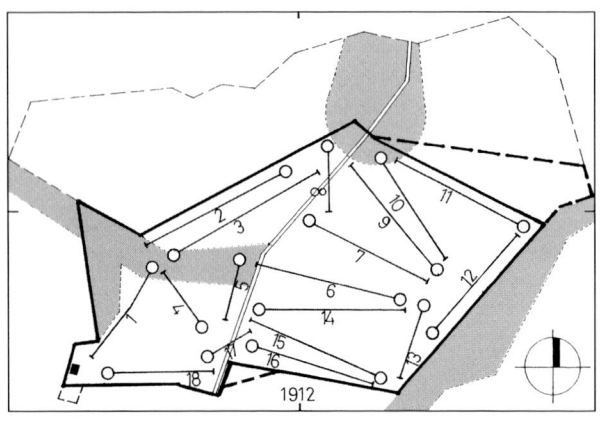

1912 Layout

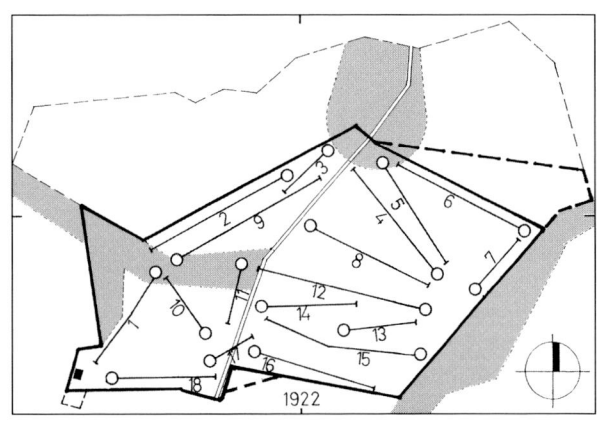

... 1922 layout ...

Inspection of the 1912 layout shows that the present holes Nos. 1, 2, 4, 5, 8 and 10 had appeared. In addition, the third green was established, albeit played from a different tee (now the ninth). Many of the holes were played in a different order from the present and it also appears that the current practice green was the fourth green of that time.

By coincidence or otherwise, for much of the winter of 1991/92 we played the eighteenth as it was in 1912, and we also appear to have played the original (1893) first hole, with the alternate winter green on the brow of the hill.

There was no further development during the Great War, but by 1922 further changes had taken place.

By this time our present 5th and 3rd greens were in existence though the 5th was played as the 10th (bottom of page) and the 8th (below) as the 3rd from what is now in the area of the 9th tee. One hole from this era the 13th (right) no longer exists and was played from the far side of the quarry at what is now the 16th to an area behind the present 14th tee.

At this time holes one to eight were in today's order, although the third was from yet another tee, and the sixth and seventh were as they remained until 1960. The thirteenth had appeared (as the twelfth) in its modern form.

In 1923 another milestone was reached when James Braid, the five times Open champion, was commissioned to make further improvements. He visited Helensburgh on Wednesday, September 26, and a signed copy of his report, dated September 29, is in the club's possession.

It may be of interest to reproduce excerpts from his report:

1st - This is an excellent hole but I consider that the fairway is too wide on the right hand side even in view of the fact that it is advisable to have a comparatively wide fairway for the first hole.

2nd - I suggest that a new tee should be constructed 26 yards behind the back of the hindmost tee thus making the hole approximately 430 yards. This would give a good drive the benefit of landing on favourable ground. I suggest a bunker on the crest of the hill 4 feet high at the right side and 3 feet high at the left, also other bunkers, one at the right and one at the left corner of the green.

3rd - Here I strongly advise that a

new tee be constructed on a level with the front of the second green and as near the fence as possible. (At the time the tee was located near the present 10th tee).

4th - here I suggest a bunker on the right 3 feet 6 inches high about midway to the hole, while immediately in front of the green I recommend that 2 feet six inches of earth be taken off the crest of the hill, making a level portion 10 yards in length . . . the material taken from this to be used in the construction of two large mounds, one at the right and the other at the left front corner of the green, the opening between these to be 14 yards wide and of irregular shape.

7th (played then from near to the present ladies' tee) - Bunkers should be constructed (1) on the right about midway to the hole 2 feet 6 inches high, (2) at the right front corner of the green 4 feet high and (3) on the left side of the green, about the middle 3 feet high.

Proposed new 9th hole - I suggest that a new hole should be constructed, having its tee behind and in the rough to the right of the old 9th tee and the green being situated on a little naturally flat surface immediately over the Old Luss Road. This in my opinion would be a good short hole.

9th (now the 10th) - I suggest a large bunker immediately at the top of the hill to the right 5 feet high on the right and 3 feet high on the left.

Suggested new holes (now the 11th and 12th) - (a) I suggest that there be a new hole having the tee in the rough, outside the second fir tree on the left of the course to the present 10th, the green being situated in the rough on a level with the trees beside of the 18th green, the green to be guarded on the right and left front by bunkers.

(b) - I suggest then that a tee be constructed at the side of the proposed new green from which the play should be to the present 11th hole . . . The whins and trees in the vicinity of the 11th green should be left as at present.

Braid suggested further changes to the remaining holes, as he did for the 6th and 7th, none of which are played today quite in the same manner. Braid did add, however: "All the holes on the higher part of the course are of a soft, peaty nature and should be thoroughly treated with ashes. In my opinion this is the only method by which any material improvement will be made in the quality of the fairway on this part of the course."

The committee of the day accepted the majority of Braid's proposals. However, they did not proceed with them all immediately, as judged by the layout contained in the 1924 handbook.

Braid introduced many of our present day bunkers and lengthened a few holes. He also fixed the third in its present day form, created the ninth and eleventh and

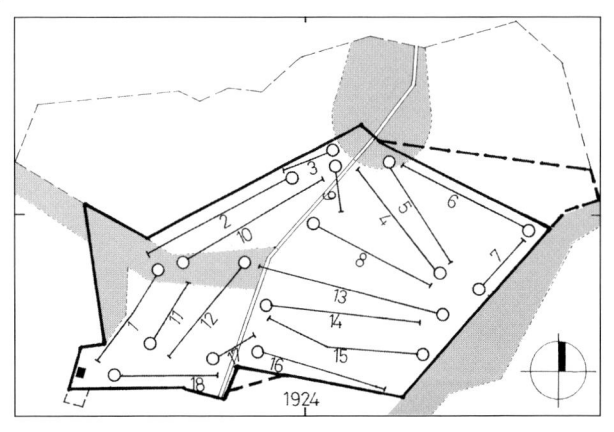

... 1924 layout ...

consolidated the twelfth and fourteenth, more or less as now played.

It is interesting to note that the reason for extending the second tee, back by some 26 yards, was to provide a better landing area for a good drive. It is safe to assume that a good drive in those days landed on the upslope and the Braid alteration was to avoid this. With today's equipment the problem of the upslope has returned.

In the 1920s bogey was the order of the day and Helensburgh, at 5,595 yards, had a bogey score of 75. There were seven bogey 5s, including the eighth at 350 yards.

The ladies, who played a shorter course, had two bogey scores, one was 77 which was played from May until September and outwith that period it was 81.

In addition it seems obvious that some bunkers which are now considered to be located in irrelevant places were more serious hazards then.

The next layout comes from a 1933 handbook, which shows the establishment of the current 16th and 17th holes. The 15th also appears, but played from a tee closer to the 17th green and the 18th played from the what is now the 15th tee.

A report in the Helensburgh and Gareloch Times of July 27, 1932, describes the new holes thus: "The new 15th presents little difficulty to the player except that the habitual slicer has to beware of the boundary hedge. The 16th, over the quarry, is 156 yards - a mashie shot, simple if you hit it clean, but if duffed trouble ensues. The 17th takes one back to the old 16th green, and at the 18th you play across the Old Luss Road to the last green, which, as yet, has not been altered owing possibly to the dissension about the crab apple tree.

There is the fascination of novelty about playing over the new layout. It may be an improvement, but it is too new to form an opinion."

That the general layout has remained to this day, with alterations to come only to holes 6 and 7 and a few tees, tends to suggest it was a great success. Whatever was the dissension over the crab apple tree, and we might surmise it had been planted in someone's memory, it was solved the following February, as, according to a report: "The construction of the new 18th hole is now proceeding. The crab apple tree, which was the subject of controversy, has now been razed."

Careful examination of the plans reveals that the 15th green has been a green and a tee and both at

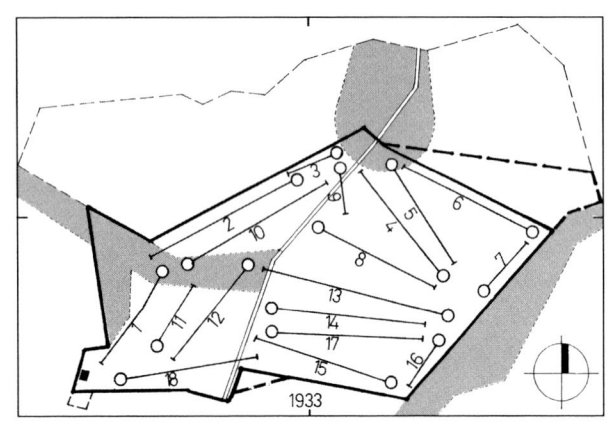

... 1933 layout ...

various times. The 18th green is still shown in the hollow below the current location. The relevant handbook still refers to the Braid changes of 1924, and yet the 1933 version does not conform to the great man's report in every respect, though he may have returned to advise.

The next layout appears in 1938, the most obvious change being to the 18th green. The 8th green was also moved south, forming the present slight dogleg. This work was carried out when R R Herbertson was greens convener, and the 1930s also saw the conversion to sand bunkers. Various minutes indicate that Herbertson was very active in the club's affairs for many years. The changes to the sixth and seventh, although not fully implemented until 1960, were planned around 1937 and these were the most significant changes to the course since the last war, made under the direction of Malcolm Grierson.

There was some thought given to playing the 5th, 6th and 7th in reverse but this idea was abandoned, and consideration was also given to a further extension to the 7th, a prospect which has been raised again in recent years by taking the tee further back and to the east to make the hole a dogleg par 5.

So, with the exception of these last two holes, the course had at last settled down.

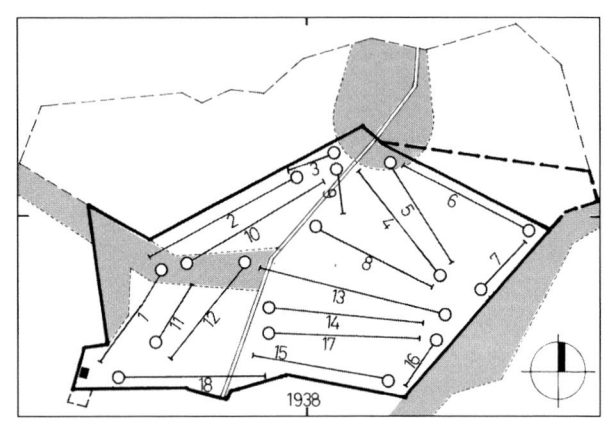

... 1938 layout ...

Without doubt there have been many detailed alterations stretching various holes from 5,656 yards (1938) to the existing 6,058 yards, and between 1924 and 1933 the bogey rules had changed, reducing the number

What is now the 15th green has been altered on several occasions. In this picture from the 1912 handbook it is shown to be both a green and a tee.

of 5s from seven to four.

One of the disappointments in reading the old records is to find that some of the original character has been removed. For example, in 1933, R H K Browning wrote: "The twelfth is 300 yards long and is one of the finest holes of its length that I have ever seen. We drive slightly uphill with a sea of gorse along our right ... "

There are other references to gorse, which was clearly there from the outset but which, sadly, has been removed at some time.

During the Second World War there was compulsory grazing on the course, and after 1945 shortages of materials and labour was a problem, especially as considerable work was needed to rectify damage caused by cattle. Efforts to find a workforce included an approach to use prisoners of war, but this was declined.

Three men eventually were employed, which was considered less than the requirement, but despite the makeshift nature of the course, including fences round all greens to keep the cattle and sheep off, the course was playable. Furthermore, probably because the rough had been kept low through grazing, there was little risk of losing balls which were in short supply. When new balls were obtained, they were awarded by ballot.

Early in 1946 a special meeting was called to discuss the future of the course, and the topics included restoration of all the greens, which had shrunk to what the new professional, Malcolm Grierson, described as "postage stamps", improvement of drainage, renewal of equipment, completion of a new 6th, and extension of the 7th. Along with other expenditure a 33% increase in the annual subscription was agreed - from three to four guineas.

The course improved the following year. A drain was was laid across the gully crossing the 13th, 14th and 15th fairways, ditches continued to be deepened and drained. Later, a new drainage system was installed on the far section of the 8th but further work on this was found necessary in the 1970s.

In 1947 compulsory grazing ended, though this returned briefly for a maximum of 60 sheep two years later by order of the Clyde Agricultural Executive Committee. The fences though were taken down, and the course was gradually returning to its pre-war condition

The 12th in those days was exceptionally prone to flooding, and in 1948 a ditch running across the 2nd and 10th, which has since been filled in, was diverted. The following year the 6th tee back in the woods was created, the shelter at the 10th erected and the triangle formed by the 12th, 18th and Old Luss Road was cleared for the practice area which remains today.

New tees were in place at the 2nd and the 7th, and the standard scratch score of 69 was sanctioned in 1951, the same year as the ditch at the 7th was filled in, and by using aerial photographs a comprehensive drainage scheme was undertaken.

In an act of great foresight, Helensburgh Golf Club bought the course from Luss Estates in February 1978, for what in hindsight must be considered a bargain price of £86,500 for the 110 acres which comprise the present course plus 60 acres to the north, working out at £500 an acre. However, the prior negotiations were of necessity conducted in secret, only three people being aware of the purchase discussions.

These were Douglas Dalgleish, the greens convener whose skills as a lawyer were even more important, Matt Kirk, the club captain, and Jim Stark, the vice-captain, and the meetings with the factor of Luss Estates, Mr. J Duberley were held in Foreland, the Dalgleish residence.

The reason for the clandestine nature of the discussions was that the factor believed the plan was likely to be scuppered if the laird, Sir Ivar Colquhoun, was to hear about it before the entire package had been put together, almost as a fait accompli. In the event Sir Ivar agreed the deal, but there was great angst among the remainder of the committee, and the members, who felt they had been left unreasonably in the dark.

"Could you not have trusted us," was the question asked, to which the answer was probably, but nothing, absolutely nothing, could be left to chance. Fourteen years after this controversial deal was struck we can view this episode more comfortably as a highly successful coup (no double meaning intended).

At that time the club had a 19-year lease on the course with rent reviewed every seven years. In 1978 this review had just taken place and Luss Estates had raised the annual rent from £300 to £2,000 and the club thought it would be wise to secure the future and buy the land outright. There had been a trend of estates moving into the commercial side of golf courses, as was threatening to happen at other locations in Scotland, and there were fears this might happen at Helensburgh.

Part of the deal was a further 60 acres of land to the north which is not yet in use though an attempt was made shortly after the purchase to clear and seed the section immediately to the north of the second fairway. It was not completed, however, and the ground has returned to its original wild state, despite a second attempt at clearance.

Today, the area looks like a wild tree nursery.

The decision to purchase was made at a special meeting of the club in the Victoria Halls, and more than half the money was raised by £100 interest-free loans from each of the 450 ordinary members, many of them paying this off at £2 a month through agreements with local banks. The remaining sum came from a bank overdraft facility.

Many of these £100 debts were written off by members in return for various privileges in 1993 as centenary patrons.

One of the more significant changes in recent years is to the 12th green, which as already noted is one of only two original 1893 locations. Much of the work on this new surface was masterminded in the 1980s by the then professional Brian Anderson, who was frequently to be seen donning wellies and out on the course, more often than not at the 12th.

That green had always been a problem and it had reached the stage of being non-repairable. A quote of £15,000 was received for its reconstruction, raising it by several feet and removing the bunker immediately in front, though Anderson was never sure that latter amendment was a good idea.

However, with his help the job was done for the £4,000 cost of the materials and using the club's own labour. It must be said that the problem of this green has not gone away, in terms of surface quality and there is a view that there has been no improvement at all.

New tees were constructed at the 7th, 10th, 12th and

The 12th green before reconstruction: Was it a mistake to remove the bunker?

15th, and with the advice of now retired agronomist Jim Arthur the course came on in leaps and bounds. Anderson also felt that the creation of another nine holes on unused land to the north and west could be created in the early 80s. This idea was taken as far as the drawing up of a layout by modern day course architect Donald Steel, a former English international player and distinguished golf writer, but was never put into effect.

One of the more recent alterations was to the sixth, where until 1980 the rough to the left which forms the dogleg was in play. The temptation to cut the corner was much more pronounced and as a result caused a bottleneck on medal days with a succession of players hunting for balls. At the suggestion of John Munro, with the idea of speeding up play, this area was declared out of bounds.

First to play the hole with the new rule in force was the so-called Dawn Patrol comprising clubmaster Gibby Beattie, who invariably teed off before 8am so that he could be back for the 11am opening of the bar, and Jim Stark, the match and handicap secretary. Stark, with the honour, reminded his playing partner to beware, and then being the first player who could possibly go out of bounds there promptly did so with a glorious hook. If Munro's ears were burning that morning it was hardly surprising as he was cursed all the way from the tee to the rough where, as a further irony, the ball was found lying well. Following this initial hiccup, however, the alteration has generally been accepted as successful and remains today.

The title of course manager, currently held by Ronnie Myles, is a new one reflecting the skills and qualifications now needed for such a career. Originally Tom Turnbull, under supervision from the greens convener, was in control although there was a greenkeeper, Andrew Park, who died in 1945 while serving with the RAF. Malcolm Grierson was the first head greenkeeper, an appointment considered more important than that of professional. A Mr Peacock held the post for some time until Eddie Boyce, the No.2, took over in 1970 and in the mid 1960s, the club bought a flat in Colquhoun Square to aid recruitment of greenkeepers, but this was later sold. One of Boyce's apprentices, John Muir, an honours graduate in horticultural sciences at Bath University, went on to become head greenkeeper at the Open Championship final qualifying venue of West Lancashire. On his retirement Boyce was replaced by John Grainger and when he left in 1991 Myles took over.

They have all battled with the biggest single problem about our course - drainage. And to prove that some things do not change, the club has in its possession a report dated December 1924 from the West of Scotland Agricultural College which begins:

"It is evident, beyond any possibility of doubt, that the course suffers from a degree of saturation which must seriously affect the playing conditions. For this state of affairs no single cause can, generally speaking, be attributed, although all courses have been aggravated by an apparent neglect of the various drainage systems over a number of years."

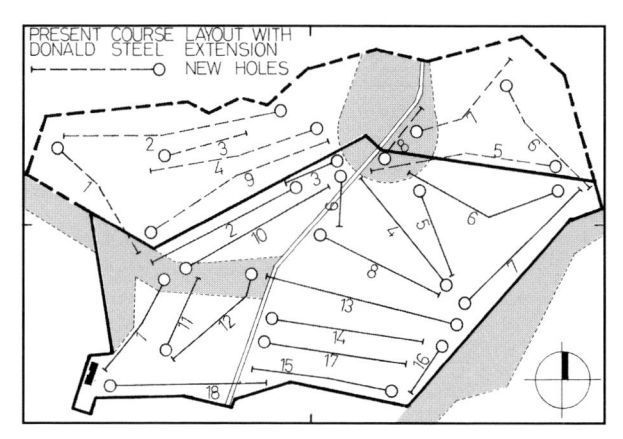

Modern layout.

As we enter our centenary year, the prospect of a major development remains open. The deal struck with the developer, namely Wimpey, embraces the sale of up to 37 acres for housing, the construction of replacement holes, a new clubhouse and hopefully the acquisition of additional ground to the north, retaining the ambition of 27 holes. There are local authority and private objections leading to public enquiry and the matter is now in the hands of the Reporter and the Secretary of State for Scotland. One must accept the merits of the democratic process but it is a pity that the vision and enthusiasm for the golfing amenity shown in 1893 does not prevail today.

The club can lay claim to having preserved natural features, for example trees, as Ian McIntyre has recently highlighted.

"Many of the trees which can be seen around the golf course were there before 1893. They have survived many storms and have witnessed with great dignity the antics of mere mortals as they have disported themselves from one little hole to another. In particular, the standing of Scots Pines on top of the hill beyond the third green contains over 1000 specimens. The Oak beside the first tee was there at the beginning, as were many of the Beeches near to the sixth tee and extending down both sides of the Old Luss Road. At least one magnificent tree is over 200 years old.

It is hoped that the centenary year will provide the impetus to assist nature, by planting trees of distinction, some for golfing reasons, some just to admire and all to continue the silent witness for the next 100 years."

JAMES BRAID
"A good eye for country"

James Braid: located many of our present day bunkers.

James Braid (1870-1950), who advised in 1923 on the redesign of the course, was born in a house on the border between Elie and Earlsferry, Fife, in 1870. He served most of his professional career in England notably at Walton Heath in Surrey, and is regarded a central figure in an era in which golf grew from a little known sport to one played the world over.

Braid's father of the same christian name was a farmer and forester, never played golf, and disapproved of young James playing golf professionally. However, the community in which he lived was obsessed by the game in the latter part of the 19th century and Braid was caught up in it. His teenage heros were players like Jack Simpson and Douglas Rolland, respectively first and second in the 1884 Open at Prestwick.

Braid, who served an apprenticeship as a joiner, became a professional golfer in 1893 when a friend offered him a job as clubmaker at a London store, the kind of job he had always longed for, from where he moved to the club job at Romford before his final posting to Walton Heath.

Braid established his playing credentials when he halved a 36-hole exhibition match against the then twice Open champion John Henry (J H) Taylor at West Drayton in 1895, and went on to become one of the so-called Great Triumvirate, all born within 13 months of each other and comprising Englishman Harry Vardon as well as Taylor and Braid.

From 1894 until the outbreak of the First World War the triumvirate won 16 Open Championships among them. When Braid won his first of five Open Championships in 1901, Taylor and Vardon each had three, but by 1910 Braid was ahead of both, the Anglo-Scot having won all of them in the country of his birth.

His first was at Muirfield using the guttie, and his next four at St Andrews (1905), Muirfield (1906), Prestwick (1908), and St Andrews (1910) were achieved with the rubber-cored Haskell ball, the last in the Jubilee Open Championship.

Braid was said to have been a powerful golfer blessed with a serene disposition. A man of few words, Braid, whose grand-daughter Mrs Marjorie Mackie presently lives in Cardross and provided us with a picture of the great man, is reputed never to have shown emotion on the course. It was said that he struck the ball in his heyday "with divine fury", though his short game was not quite so natural, especially his putting at which he had to work hard.

It was in the latter part of his career, when playing commitments lessened, that he took to course architecture. The most famous course Braid designed is the King's Course at Gleneagles Hotel. Others in which he had a hand either designing or, like Helensburgh, altering, include Carnoustie, Blairgowrie, Dalmahoy, Belleisle, Buchanan Castle, Hilton Park, Greenock, Forfar and many others in England.

Bernard Darwin, in his biography of Braid, wrote of his architecture: "I should not say that he was very imaginative or subtle in the designing of a hole - and it is possible to be too subtle for ordinary human nature - but he had what the good architect needs, a good eye for country and, as in everything that he touched, a temperate judgment and a fund of plain common sense.

"We hear a great deal of the contrast between the penal and strategic schools of architecture and I do not propose to become involved in any discussion on that thorny question. I do not think that James was deliberately penal in spotting bunkers here and there to catch each and all of the bad shots. He was much too good an artist for that, but at the same time he did not like to let the errant player "get away with it," and would now and again have a gently malign satisfaction in blocking his too wide and easy road."

These comments could be applied to some of the bunkers, recommended in his 1923 report on Helensburgh, and which survive today, including the one at the top of the hill at the 2nd which prevents the scuttled shot from being successful. He also advised on the bunkers to the right and left of the 2nd green. The bunker in the rough to the right of the 4th fairway to catch the sliced tee shot was also Braid's idea.

We know who to blame now, but even though we might have cause to curse James Braid from time to time, his name, like that of Old Tom Morris, adds considerably to the prestige of our club history.

CHAPTER 3

The two clubhouses

THE NINETEENTH: NEVER WITHOUT ITS LOOPHOLES

THE original clubhouse, known as "The Tin Hut", was situated in 1894 just to the west of the Old Luss Road. The original estimate of its cost was £150, amended later to £200 and the reality was £295. In its first year it was insured for 16/3d (about 82p).

The building, constructed of wood and corrugated iron, was described as commodious and elegant and fitted up with the usual boxes for members and with well-arranged retiring rooms. It also had a ladies' room fitted out similarly to the men's - further evidence that Helensburgh has been a family-type club from the outset.

Furniture and fittings cost a further £50 15/7d, but some tools were included in this value almost certainly to maintain the course.

This clubhouse, which was upgraded to include more windows and relocated in 1900 close to the West Highland Railway Line in Abercromby Street for reasons of easier access, served the members for 15 years and in 1909 "The Tin Hut" was sold to G Galbraith of Dumbarton for £35 "without lockers, stove, sink and wash-hand basins" which were to be retained. We presume that Galbraith was acting for the Vale of Leven Golf Club.

The old house was acquired by Vale of Leven Golf

Two golfers complete with caddies about to tee off at the original first against the background of the "Tin Hut" in its original location by the Old Luss Road.

The modified "Tin Hut" in its second location in Abercromby Street.

Club, whose records tell us that their new pavilion was erected for £99 10/- in June, 1910, and parts of this building were still in service in the 1970s. It is possible that the affinity between Helensburgh and Vale of Leven arose at that time and Vale members were most supportive of our 1974 pro-am, providing many volunteers to assist on the day.

In 1908 the Helensburgh committee resolved to build a new clubhouse, and a number of old documents and papers have been found relating to the costs in 1909 of constructing the clubhouse which forms the basis of the one in use at the present time and these have been examined by Alex Brownlie to whom we are grateful for the following analysis:

"These documents consist mainly of final account measurements for the trades involved in the construction of a "Club House at Golf Course, Upper Helensburgh, done for the Directors of Helensburgh Golf Club."

The measurements also include the work in constructing a "Caddies' House" which appears to have consisted largely of a bicycle shed and a repair shop with a minimal amount of living accommodation.

Of the nine contractors who participated in the project, two at least are still in business. These are James Grant (now trading as J Grant (Builders) Ltd., of 290 Pinkston Road, Glasgow), who undertook the carpenter, joiner, ironmonger and glazier works, and J W Guthrie and Andrew Wells Ltd. (now trading as Guthrie and Wells Ltd., of 580 Lawrence Street, Glasgow), who carried out the painting.

Those who no longer appear to be in business were: John Jack (digger, mason and brickworks), P & W McLellan Ltd. (steelwork), P White & Company (roughcasting), R A McGilvray & Ferris (plaster work), William Thom & Son (slater work), Steel & Wilson (plumber and gasfitter work), J G Walker & Sons (asphalt work).

The final measurements themselves are handwritten on 13" by 8" (approx.) sheets of custom ruled measurement paper similar, apart from size, to those used by many quantity surveying practices today, and each trade measurement is individually hand-bound with pink ribbon. The art of pink ribbon binding was one of the first skills acquired by an apprentice measurer and surveyor in those days and for many years afterwards.

The measurers in this case were Myers and Brown, a firm which like many of the contractors does not appear to have survived.

According to the final accounts which were certified as correct by a firm named Mitchell and Whitelaw (architects), the total cost of construction amounted to £2,487 4/9d (£2,487.24p). Professional fees would probably have raised this to around £2,700 showing a saving of about 3% against the budget of £2,780 - changed days indeed!

No standard method of measurement was available in 1909/10 when the clubhouse final measurements were being prepared, nor indeed when the original Schedules of Quantities were prepared even earlier for the purpose of obtaining competitive tenders.

It is interesting to note therefore the similarity between the methods of measurement adopted in the clubhouse documents and those laid down some six years later in the Scottish Mode for the Measurement of Building Works, although the latter did rationalise and standardise the procedure.

The quantities were calculated and stated in Duo-Decimals, a magical system which accommodated the complexities of imperial measurements and the old currency of LSD (no, not the drug, just pounds, shillings and pence). Alas, the Duo-Decimal is no more, having succumbed to metrication and decimalisation.

Other papers located within the final account documents include a list of all the quotations received in connection with the painter work contract and details of the china and glass supplied for the catering needs of the clubhouse.

Among the painting contractors who submitted unsuccessful bids were Robert Carson (now trading as R P Carson, of 62 John Street) and I W McCulloch (better known today as I L B McCulloch, of Colquhoun Square). Ian assures us he is more competitive than was his great grandfather.

The china and glass were supplied by R & A Urie (still located in West Clyde Street). The order included some 300 items of crockery, 126 assorted glasses, 24 teapots, 36 large jugs, 24 egg cups and 48 individual dishes, bowls and jugs of various sizes, all for the princely sum of £10 19/- (£10.95p). There is no truth in the rumour that Ann and Tom Ring fell heir to this fine collection, nor is it true that it now graces the dining room at Western Gailes, the new domain of former clubmaster Gibby Beattie.

There are, of course, no documents relating to electrical works for fairly obvious reasons. Lighting was provided by gas lanterns with incandescent burners and globes. A paper found with the documents lists the quantities and distribution of 12 pendants and 27 wall brackets with prices totalling all of £23.

The documents are, not surprisingly, full of examples too numerous to mention of the incredibly low prices of those days (or so they seem now). One item, however, which may be of interest is the flagpole described as being 39 feet long, complete with 8" diameter standard, brass pulleys, copper wire, cord, yacht hooks and malleable iron straps, and all for £7 including erection.

Money to pay for this clubhouse, which was opened in 1909, by the Duke of Argyll, was raised by debentures, the last of which were repaid some 40 years later."

All present and correct for the formal opening, on what obviously was a cold day, of the new clubhouse on October 16, 1909, by the Duke of Argyll.

The clubhouse as it is today.

With this brand new, five-star clubhouse you might have thought that the old corrugated iron model might have been forgotten quickly. Nostalgia, however, grew and 27 years after its relocation at Vale of Leven one of the first Helensburgh Golf Club societies was formed. It was called the "Tin House Club". This club's records are still in existence, and we reprint its own handwritten story:

"The idea of the "Tin House Club" originated in a competition among a number of Tom Turnbull's old friends to celebrate the thirtieth anniversary of his coming as professional to Helensburgh Golf Club.

The competition was a great success and a number of other similar competitions followed, but there was no thought of the affair being an annual one until 1932 when Mr. George R Murray offered to present a medal

The "Tin House Club" meeting of June 8, 1937: Back row (l to r) J McElroy, R Stanton, W K MacLachlan, W Easton, A McCulloch, A Douglas, S Mackay. Middle - R Calder, A Stewart, G R Murray, J Miller, A McDougall, W Ferguson, T Turnbull. Front - S Brown, W M Bryden, R Ness, A Gordon.

HELENSBURGH GOLF CLUB CENTENARY

for annual competition.

This generous offer was accepted and as the original competitors had been members of the Helensburgh Golf Club in the days when the clubhouse was an erection of wood and corrugated iron with a corrugated iron roof known familiarly as the "Tin House" or "Tin Shanty", it seemed most appropriate that the medal should be called the Tin House Medal."

The clubhouse referred to was originally situated west of the Old Luss Road near the old seventeenth green. It was later removed to the site now occupied by Gemmill's house, and is now doing service with Vale of Leven Golf Club.

At a meeting in 1936 it was suggested that a kind of club might be formed with a simple constitution. This was unanimously agreed to and the following constitution was adopted:

1. The club shall be called "The Tin House Club."
2. Membership shall be confined to members of Helensburgh Golf Club who were members of that club during the existence of the "Tin House" and to other members of that club who may be duly proposed and seconded and approved of by the majority of the members of "The Tin House Club" present at the annual gathering or by the committee.
3. Each member on admission shall take an oath de fideli and sign the membership roll.
4. Members failing to attend any meetings duly convened without a valid excuse shall be fined in the sum of One Shilling Scots which shall be credited to the funds of this club.
5. A bogey competition followed by a supper shall be held each year on a date to be fixed by the committee.
6. The winner of the competition shall be entitled to hold for the ensuing year the medal presented by Mr. George R Murray and shall be elected captain of the club for the ensuing year.
7. A committee consisting of a secretary and two other members shall also be elected annually at the annual gathering and shall make arrangements for the next meeting with power to adjust handicaps. The captain shall be a member of the committee ex officio.

There was also a form of declaration for new entrants which indicates that the dilemmas faced by the modern golfer, namely dereliction of duty at home and, on the course, the question of banditry, were the same then as they are now. It read:

You promise and declare that you will be a faithful member of this club and despite the solicitations of wife, children, sweethearts, or friends, you undertake to attend regularly all duly convened meetings. Illness and the demands of business being alone valid excuses for absence.

You further undertake not to endeavour by bribes, promises, or threats to procure a sympathetic handicap for any of the competitions promoted by the club.

In token of the members appreciation of the solemnity of the obligation undertaken he will kiss the brick."

Whether or not the solicitations of wife, children etc. ultimately prevailed, "The Tin House Club" appears to have been active for no more than two years and the annual competition of Friday, June 24, 1938, at which 17 members were present, is the last one recorded. Nevertheless, we have clear evidence of an early clique, another tradition which continues.

The clubhouse has served the membership well as the basic structure remains, though extensions were completed in 1965 and again in 1973. However, there have been problems of leakage from time to time and, arguably, the future requires us to think of a new building.

In 1965 Alan Christianson, then captain and now president of the club, formally opened a £16,000 extension which enclosed the original verandah and extended the inside walls outwards by some ten feet to a design by architect and captain-to-be Ian Plenderleath. The additional space was used to provide a men's lounge, mixed lounge and a larger dining room, all with picture windows taking advantage of the splendid views. By providing a mixed lounge the social pattern of the club was also changed.

In 1973 the rear of the original structure was extended and some of the advantages were locker accommodation to meet the needs of increased membership, new toilet facilities, an internal professionals' shop and provision for juniors. A new men's bar freed the entire front of the house to become a mixed lounge.

The balcony enclosure above the mixed lounge and dining room was a 1980s construction consistent with the 1965 phase 2 proposals to remove the flat roof problem. Given the superb high-level view it is a pity that this phase was never fully completed.

The latest development was the sumptuous £60,000 refurbishment (compare that to £295 in 1894 for an entire clubhouse) of the mixed lounge in 1989 which has encouraged a big increase in the use of the clubhouse.

A contrast in style: above is the mixed lounge as it is today while alongside (top right) is the ladies room and (bottom right) the gentlemen's reading and smoking room as they were in the 1930s.

There are few records which throw any light on clubhouse usage and functions before the 1950s, although visiting clubs were invariably said to have been impressed with the hospitality. On medal days, however, some older members recall the lounge being a very quiet place in which those who had just moved up from the junior ranks were frightened even to cough. Decorum was very much the thing, and in the dining room, afternoon tea with silver service was quite an elaborate affair. Despite this air of respectability, there is no doubt whatsoever that alcohol was consumed, as Alex Parker found when he examined club minute books which survive from the late forties. He relates:

"At the end of World War II spirits, like everything else, were rationed. The club received a quota, presumably based on membership or perhaps "influence" and members were allowed one glass of whisky or gin per day. The exception appears to have been the day of the annual general meeting when rationing was lifted until the start of proceedings. No mention is made in the minutes of whether this was to stimulate attendance and debate or to befuddle the argumentative.

Other exceptions were less specific, but one report recorded: "The scarcity of supplies of spirituous liquor compelled rationing, but judging from the turnover at the bar this scheme has not been without loopholes."

It is understood that around this time the local minister, who liked his dram, had his ration served in a glass of milk to avoid criticism from his parishioners.

In February, 1946, the daily ration was increased to two glasses of whisky with half a glass of gin and one glass of beer per member, such quotas to be shared with guests. Three months later, following what was surprisingly referred to as the healthy consumption of whisky at the club, the quota was reduced. However, by September, restrictions on beer were lifted.

As one can imagine, considerable care was taken to monitor supplies, and on April 20, 1947, a sad day for the club, it was discovered that a bottle of gin contained water. A Mr. David Laverock - not previously appearing in club minutes, although one assumes a member - "kindly agreed to inspect and test the remaining stock."

It was reported to the committee some two months later that the entire stock had been tested and found to be in order. Nice work if you can get it.

Gin rationing ended in September that year, but whisky continued to be restricted for some time thereafter."

The clubhouse appears to have been adequate to host the membership at modest size events and while the dinner to mark Morty Dykes' Scottish Amateur success in 1951 was taken to Shandon Hydro it seems that only in the 1970s did it become necessary to go elsewhere for annual and special general meetings. Bear in mind though that the agm was at one time held on a Saturday at 4pm to be followed immediately by the annual prize-giving. The bar, unlike the immediate post-war era, was closed at the appointed hour and typically the entire proceedings lasted an hour. The separation of these events has without doubt caused both of them to last longer and the clubhouse can no longer host the vociferous and spirited agm. Before 1973 the agm took place in a space roughly one third of the mixed lounge and the table, complete with trophies and committee, occupied a significant part of the available space.

During the 1960s the social use of the clubhouse expanded considerably under the direction of an active social sub-committee. The main event was a monthly Friday evening dance which was extraordinarily well attended. There was one occasion in the 1970s when the Christmas dance had some 240 people through the door. Intimacy, as a result, was more than usual with dancing partners having to hold each other very closely because of the cramped conditions. Some members, however, do not appear to have enjoyed themselves because a vote was taken at the next agm to reduce the number of guests per member. As a result the whole busy scene evaporated, never to recover.

The annual dinner dance took place in those days in the now defunct Queens Hotel but the unfortunate habit of committee members hogging the tickets caused the social sub-committee to run a rival function at the Ardencaple Hotel.

Other successful endeavours have emerged over the years. There is a regular winter bridge session on Monday evenings and the ladies have organised their own one on Wednesdays. The ladies also have an annual bridge and whist evening, sewing club, mixed foursomes evening and other functions such as fashion shows, antique evenings and films.

Indoor carpet bowls was started by John Munro, at one time a successful outdoor bowler, and the Tuesday evening matches are well supported, attracting some forty participants during the winter months. In addition there are matches with local bowling clubs.

One armed bandits have been a feature of the club for at least two decades, bringing in a vital and ever growing revenue, though there is a record in the minutes of 1963 of such an idea being rejected. Some members, hooked on this indoor sport which seems to become more elaborate each year, might wish this decision was still in force.

The first machine was a tanner mechanical machine with a handle, and when the £5 jackpot paid out it was a common sight for ladies to lose their dignity and shovel the outpouring sixpences into their handbags. Nowadays the microchip ensures that the £100 jackpot is dispensed in a more orderly, though no less noisy, fashion.

The jackpot, however, has never been of a sufficient sum to cover a year's subscription and some words relating to fees for ordinary members over the years is worth including.

The initial fee was one guinea and the same amount for entrance, but there were also a number of £5 debenture holders. These remained in 1939 and probably beyond, repayments being made by ballot. By 1926 members were paying three guineas and these levels remained in place until 1947, inflation not in those days being the evil it is now. Then, there was an increase to four guineas and by 1969 it had reached 15 guineas. With the onset of the modern phenomenon of real inflation we are all aware of the position today.

Life membership has been available on occasions and in the 1920s there was no restriction when there was a flat rate of £30. In the 1930s the number of life members was limited to 30. Since then there has been a

---

HELENSBURGH GOLF CLUB.

LYNCLUTHA,
HELENSBURGH, *December 22nd, 1894.*

DEAR SIR OR MADAM,

The FIRST ANNUAL MEETING of the CLUB will be held in the MUNICIPAL CHAMBERS on THURSDAY, 27th December, at 7.45 P.M., to receive a Statement of Accounts as annexed hereto, to elect Office bearers and Committee for ensuing year, and transact any other competent business.

I have also to intimate that your subscription and rent of box as undernoted should now be paid to Mr A. M. M. G. KIDSTON, Clydesdale Bank, Helensburgh. If you have not yet paid for your box for last year, kindly do so now.

The Committee have thought it right to insure the contents of Members' Boxes for a maximum of £2 each.

It falls to the Members at this meeting to fix the amount of Debentures to be paid off, and draw the numbers by ballot.

Your obedient servant,

JOHN M. MURRAY,
Hon. Secy.

SUBSCRIPTIONS.

Ordinary Members,	£1 1 0
Lady ,,	0 10 6
Junior ,,	0 10 6
Rent of Boxes,	0 2 6

The first annual general meeting, as shown above, was held before the end of December when the financial year ended only on November 11. Nowadays, in the era of the microchip and when the financial year closes on October 31, it is sometimes a struggle to have the books ready in time for an agm at the end of January.

tendency to remove the option except on special occasions. The last one was in 1973 when the club was seeking capital funds for the clubhouse extension. There is, of course, a constitutional route to life membership based on age and length of membership.

served by the appointed moment whereupon the hatch was slammed shut leaving two very thirsty golfers.

A short lived series of appointments followed, one so short that the chosen never arrived and the committee had to begin again. Mr and Mrs C Thomson were here

HELENSBURGH GOLF CLUB.

Abstract Statement of Accounts from Formation of Club to 11th November, 1894.

I.—CAPITAL ACCOUNT.

RECEIPTS.		PAYMENTS.	
1.—Debentures—		1—Club-House, Cost,	£295 0 0
49 Debentures of £5 each,	£245 0 0	2.—Furniture and Fittings, and Tools,	50 15 7
2.—Entry-Money—		3.—Laying off Ground,	108 5 10
191 Ordinary Members at £1 1s, £200 11 0		4.—Balance in Bank,	58 13 7
89 Lady ,, at 10s 6d, 46 14 6			
8 Lady ,, at £1 1s, 8 8 0			
23 Junior ,, at 10s 6d, 12 1 6			
	267 15 0		
	£512 15 0		£512 15 0

II.—REVENUE ACCOUNT.

1.—Subscriptions—		1.—Rent and Taxes,	£63 17 11½
191 Ordinary Members at £1 1s, £200 11 0		2.—Groundman and Assistants,	78 4 9
97 Lady ,, at 10s 6d, 50 18 6		3.—Stationery and Advertising,	24 6 0
23 Junior ,, at 0s 6d, 12 1 6		4.—Expenses of Opening Day,	11 0 0
	£263 11 0	5.—Sundries, Petties, Postages, &c.,	11 3 0
2.—Visitors—		6.—Balance in Bank and on Hand,	96 2 7½
10 Weekly, at 5s, £2 10 0			
23 Monthly, at 10s, 12 10 0			
	15 0 0		
3.—Keys of House Sold,	5 0 0		
4.—Interest from Bank,	1 3 4		
	£284 14 4		£284 14 4

III.—DEBENTURE INTEREST ACCOUNT.

1.—Rent of Boxes,	£11 15 0	1.—Insurance of House,	£0 16 3
		2.—Interest to 11th November, 1894,	8 0 0
		3.—Balance in Bank,	2 18 9
	£11 15 0		£11 15 0

For half the history of the club Tom Turnbull, or should we say Mrs Turnbull, was in charge of the clubhouse and although no anecdotes about them have been forthcoming it is known they were held in high esteem.

Their son Guy took over as steward for a brief time but this was unsuccessful and ended in bitterness. This was especially sad for the parents, who held the fort again.

Mr and Mrs D Young were appointed but again did not last long. After some persuasion, the Griersons took over in 1949, so for a few years until 1954, the club had reverted to the same overall concept of the professional doing everything.

The next incumbents were Mr and Mrs Alec McKenzie, who served until 1964. These were the days of the famous hatch, through which all drink was dispensed and we are told that McKenzie's time-keeping was so precise that when a fourball was being served near to closing time, only the first two drinks were

for two years, followed by Mr. and Mrs G R McGregor, then Mr. and Mrs Gray.

Mr and Mrs Sandy Kelly appeared in 1969 and they continued successfully until 1975. Mr and Mrs Craig Reid took over and when they decided to depart in 1977, the club opted to appoint a club manager, Mr K Angus. He operated as secretary and clubmaster, assisted by his wife, but although the concept had merit, 1979 saw the termination of the arrangement.

The arrival of Gibby and Maureen Beattie brought a new approach and the enthusiasm to make better use of the clubhouse facilities. As noted elsewhere, the trio of Beattie, Phoenix and Anderson provided a professional approach to the entire operation but as with all good things they came to an end.

Late in 1991, Gibby and Maureen moved on and Tom and Ann Ring arrived to continue the impossible task of trying to keep all of the members happy all of the time.

No account of Helensburgh Golf Club would be

complete without reference to the Burns Supper. To date it has never been held on the birthday of the great man, but the quality of the event started high and has never diminished. Gordon Hanning and Douglas Dalgleish are the responsible persons and invariably participate in various ways.

The Burns Supper is a major event, usually in mid-February. There is always a toast to the game of golf but only because the nineteenth hole is the venue. The Captain's Prayer, which is featured below to conclude this chapter, was written and delivered by captain Tom Inglis (with apologies to Robert Burns) for the 1992 supper, and for those who are unfamiliar with Burns, is based on Holy Willie's Prayer.

THE CAPTAIN'S PREYER

O thou that in the Heavens does dwell,
Wha as it pleases, best thysel,
When on oor course puts us through Hell,
In search of glory,
Has sent me here this nicht tae tell,
this Gowf Club's story.

Lord, bless thy chosen in this place,
For gowfers are a special race,
Tho some in here are quite twa-faced,
Aboot their games.
But I've nae wish tae bring disgrace,
By namin names.

When from my mither's womb I fell,
She little dreamt this tale I'd tell,
Being captain of a gowf club - swell,
Could be sae nice.
Lord, send yon members a tae Hell,
Wi their advice.

Off 22 seems fair and ample,
Twa Winter League wins for example,
Tho John, my handicap wad trample,
He musna tamper.
Or else I fear I'll nae mair sample,
Yon lawyers' hamper.

Some members play wi matchless might,
McCathie huge, Dalgleish sae slight,
They strike yon ball far frae oor sight,
Wi power and grace.
We're sure, o Lord, it's hardly right,
And in bad taste.

Whit were they, or their generation,
That they should get sic exaltation,
Tae us it's just a great vexation.
There should be laws,
For them to play till their damnation,
Wi lead filled baas!

Lord, hear my earnest cry and prayer,
Against yon Coffee Club through there,
It's named because a laugh's sae rare,
The Greetin Meetin,
All sent out by their wives I swear,
Tae save the heatin.

And yin o them I maun avow,
Is diggin' up oor archives now,
Through mony a weary page he'll plough,
Stark is that man!
Tho time he finds I know not how,
Wi yon chip van.

Our cliques, O Lord, aye want tae crow,
About the mischief that they sow,
But a their secrets I'll soon know,
And whit they plan,
I'll join them, ex-officio,
As captains can.

Lord, mind Jim Barrowman's deserts,
His tongue strikes fear in members' hairts,
They'd sooner be in other pairts,
As he by stealth,
Sae gently on yon White Shield stairts,
And clears the shelf!

Lord, yon weight watchin' is a curse,
As Frank and Jim, their temperance nurse,
Such righteousness, at us, they thrust!
It seems sae silly,
Since they gied up their gin they're worse,
Than Holy Willie.

Lord, see they notes Dalgleish is makin',
My vera heart and flesh are quakin'
He smiles as I stand, sweatin', shakin',
An pish'd wi dread,
For he the last word will be takin',
I'm aff my head.

Lord he's committed deeds maist sair,
The latest brocht us tae despair,
This picture's proof I need nae mair,
Tae pass a fine,
He sat upon the President's chair,
Lord, whit a crime.

Whit a crime: in fact Douglas Dalgleish is committing a total of three.
1. Sitting in the President's Chair.
2. Dressed improperly for the men's lounge.
3. Being caught in this photograph by Jim Stark.
The club mascot, Nelson, is a non-objector.

Lord, Hanning wi his pals tonight,
Has gien committees mony a fright,
They aye must play at first daylight,
Enough's enough!
If there's nae times, don't bloody write,
Just take the huff!

His locker stinks, ye hear him cry,
For Kit-e-Kat lies close nearby,
A feline motion (he did spy),
Lord, fancy that!
But Gordon, turn a Nelson's eye,
On yon wee cat.

In answer tae this captain's prayer,
Shadow Committees are nae mair,
Ye ken, O Lord, they're hardly fair,
Aye sowin' seeds!
Lord visit them, and dinna spare,
For their misdeeds.

But Lord, remember me and mine,
Provide us with a course sublime,
But hurry Lord, there's little time,
Centenary's ben,
When a the glory shall be thine,
Amen, amen.

CHAPTER 4

The professionals

MASTERS OF ALL TRADES

HELENSBURGH has had only five club professionals covering a span of 98 years beginning in 1895 with Tom Turnbull, by far the longest servant with 51 years until his retirement in 1946. There followed Malcolm Grierson (1946-1967), Brian Anderson (1968-1986), Iain Laird (1986-1989) and our present Robert Farrell.

Turnbull and Grierson were very much in the traditional mould of professional, assuming responsibilities for the course as well as some of the tasks like teaching which are more associated with modern pros. Brian Anderson, whose contribution to professional golf has extended far beyond club level, marked the transition and his work in improving training standards for young professionals has helped to produce today's generation of club pros like Iain Laird and our present professional Robert Farrell, who are not so much club employees as businessmen in their own right.

This chapter takes a look at all five plus there are profiles of two ex-Helensburgh members, Martin Gray and Gary Orr, who have met with considerable success as tournament players, and Graham Ross who has also entered the paid ranks.

Two years after the founding of the golf club, Helensburgh appointed its first professional, Tom Turnbull, who was to remain for more than half the period of existence of the club.

Turnbull, from North Berwick, had served his apprenticeship under Ben Sayers. In comparison with his home course, Helensburgh was a wilderness which, when he arrived in the first instance he had difficulty finding. In an old booklet on the club it was recorded "that he did not know where to find the clubhouse, but he had an idea and took a cab from the station up the rough, bumpy Old Luss Road and the cabby deposited him at his destination where he was met by the late Mr Sinclair, the dentist and a popular member."

After this inauspicious start he was to make Helensburgh Golf Club his lifetime's work not least in supervising the extension to 18 holes in 1905. An article

Tom Turnbull: Helensburgh's longest serving professional in the style of the early part of the century - jacket, tie, bunnet and handlebar moustache.
Picture courtesy of Walter Bryden.

in the Helensburgh and Gareloch Times to mark 35 years with the club read: "That event (the extension) might be said to mark the beginning of an era of importance and prosperity for the club, in which the duties of professional were becoming more and more exacting.

It is one of the most fortunate circumstances of the Helensburgh club that from the time he joined it, the "pro" has always been equal to the demands made upon his services, and his valuable experience was much sought and greatly relied upon when alterations and improvements were made to the course from time to time."

In addition to laying out Helensburgh, Turnbull also had a hand in Newtonmore and Cowal, and was asked for advice about many others.

Although we have no records of him having won any tournaments of note, he was undoubtedly a top class player, having twice gone round Helensburgh in 67, and having a record of seven holes in one.

He played against the 1883 Open Champion, Willie Fernie, in an exhibition match to mark the opening of a course at Tarbet, and the match finished all square. In 1905 he also played in an exhibition match to mark the opening of the course at Garelochhead, partnering Helensburgh member John Dingwall against Mr. Daniels, the professional at Cardross, and Mr McElroy, another Helensburgh member.

His son and daughter were also good golfers. Son Guy at one time held the amateur course record at Helensburgh of 77. Mrs Turnbull was also a familiar figure at the club, assisting her husband in the duties of professional which in those days extended to greenkeeper and clubmaster as well. Their hours were said to have been dawn to dusk and there is evidence that Turnbull carried out his duties to the letter.

In 1933 he refused Lady Colquhoun permission to play the course within prohibited hours on a Saturday as per constitution - no women, and that includes ladies. The minutes books we have record that the captain of the day, James Miller, made a gallant but unsuccessful attempt to retrieve the situation and the secretary was instructed to make an apology on behalf of the club to Sir Iain. No blame was attached to Turnbull "who had merely adhered to the constitution."

Turnbull was regarded as a first class teacher and among his pupils were Ian Campbell, who was a prominent golfer in Oxford-Cambridge University matches and Tom Lunan, who at one time held a record of 31 for nine holes at St Andrews.

His period of tenure at Helensburgh is long enough ago for many members to be totally unaware of the extent of his service to the club, which in length and perhaps other aspects as well, may never be equalled.

Turnbull was succeeded in 1946 by Malcolm Grierson who arrived from Lesmahagow and was very much in the same mould as his predecessor by taking charge of management of the course as well as running a shop, where he was highly skilled in the art of club repairs, and teaching. As an amateur he had been a scratch player before turning to golf as a profession in which he was better known as a first-class teacher than a player although he did play regularly in pro-ams which at the time was a requirement of membership of the Professional Golfers' Association. Among his pupils was the 1951 Scottish Amateur champion "Morty" Dykes, who paid public tribute to his mentor immediately after his success.

The basis of his teachings are remembered as the one-piece takeaway a la Henry Cotton, and he also had an unfailing eye for a flaw, possessing the ability of

Malcolm Grierson: an outstanding teacher who possessed the ability of instant diagnosis.
Picture courtesy of John Munro.

instant diagnosis after a single swing of the club which might actually have lost him business. Some members were said to have taken advantage of this attribute by asking what they were doing wrong without booking a lesson and Grierson was ever willing to offer free advice in this manner.

If Turnbull had the greatest influence on the course, then Grierson was not far behind and in his 21 years at the club he recognised the vital importance to the course of drainage to which he paid detailed and regular attention. He also supervised the only major change to the course since the Second World War, and that was the alteration of the sixth to a dogleg and lengthening backwards of the seventh to the back tee in its present location.

He made other minor alterations and the story is still told that he installed the little pot bunker which existed until 1992 at the front right edge of the fifth green after losing the hole in a bounce game to his son in law John Munro who had played a little chip-and-run shot to set up a birdie. Grierson suggested the shot had been thinned, and on being shown the club that had been played and realising the shot was intended he located the bunker there to ensure Munro could not play the shot again. It is worth noting that our new course manager Ronnie Myles removed that bunker in 1992 and Munro is looking forward to the new turf maturing so that once again he can play a chip-and-run second - if, with his now advanced years, he can still get his tee shot far enough up.

Grierson retired in 1967 because of failing eyesight after 21 years in the job to be replaced by Brian Anderson, who was professional at Helensburgh between 1968 and 1986 before moving east to become professional and then golf director at Dalmahoy Golf and Country Club where his most visible responsibility in 1992 was the smooth running of the outstandingly successful Solheim Cup match in which the women professionals of Europe defeated their American counterparts.

Born in Lossiemouth, his golf career began with Jimmy MacKenzie at the Moray club, after whom Anderson's son is named. MacKenzie's skills as one of the last makers of hickory shafted clubs were passed on to Anderson, who continues this now extremely rare craft as a hobby whenever the scarce component parts are available.

He then moved to the Scotscraig club at Tayport, and, curiously, the contact with Helensburgh happened as a result of his clubmaking. He was supplying Low's sports shop in Dundee, whose proprietor Millar Low was a friend of the then Helensburgh vice-captain, Douglas Lowe, originally from Arbroath.

At that time, in the late sixties, the club was looking not only for a replacement for Malcolm Grierson, but someone to help take the club into a new era as the first professional without greenkeeping duties, and to form part of a club management team effectively as golf manager.

Millar suggested to Lowe that Anderson might be the man for the job and was duly interviewed. Anderson was at first sceptical that such a set-up would be commercially viable, but was eventually convinced and made the move which was to have a tremendous impact on the club over his 18 years' tenure.

At that time the shop, at the side of the first tee, was a separate building which Anderson remembers as having plenty of character with a flagstone floor, character windows and a pleasant atmosphere. The workshop was small, but adequate.

With hindsight Anderson feels that he might have mixed that traditional character with modern fittings, but in any case the business was developing to the point that it was outgrowing the size of the shop. An extension to the clubhouse was being planned, and part of this development was to have the professional's shop as an integral part.

The original plan had the shop front in line with the locker room, but Anderson, drawing upon his hitherto hidden knowledge of architecture, argued the point that the building would look better if the shop front was in line with the men's lounge. That, of course, would also mean more space for the shop although this was never part of his case, which he won cunningly.

Anderson had further been working at strengthening the ladies and juniors sections by arranging group lessons, involving as many as 30 ladies, some of whom are the established members of today, and on Saturday mornings for juniors.

The management side of affairs was carried out in partnership with clubmaster Gibby Beattie, and Bert Phoenix in the financial role, a trio who turned out to be an extremely effective team, broken up only by Bert's death and he was never replaced. On Anderson's part this involved, among other things, refining the booking system for tee-off times and dispensing with the ball chute, until then the means of organising the order (when your ball reached the bottom of the chute it was your turn) and introducing a system which, on medal days, remains.

This was the club's first advance booking system and operates on the basis of guaranteed times within 40 minute periods, each of which accommodate five groups of three.

Brian Anderson: the first of Helensburgh's modern professionals.
Picture courtesy of The Herald.

Latterly Anderson did revert to an involvement with the course, like Turnbull and Grierson before him, His contribution is included in the section on the course's evolution.

Anderson has never been an outstanding player though he did win one West of Scotland PGA championship - but he can still claim to have had custody of all the West trophies at the same time. That was when he was the captain of the West at the time it was merged into the Scottish Region of the PGA. As a result he was responsible for all the silverware, which was locked in a bank vault in Helensburgh before the journey to The Belfry, where they are now on permanent display.

Then, on the nomination of Glasgow's Jack Steven, he became Scottish captain in 1980, bringing further honour to the club beyond which Anderson has made an immense contribution, particularly in the training of young professionals, having set up the original residential training courses along with Sandy Jones, then the Scottish Region secretary, and Jack Barrie, mine host at Powfoulis Manor, where they were held. The courses are now held at Inverclyde, but prior to the Powfoulis initiative assistants had to travel to England for instruction.

Anderson was made an honorary member when he left, and has since kept in touch regularly with the club.

A young Iain Laird during his term at Helensburgh as an assistant.

One of his assistants during his 18 years at Helensburgh was Iain Laird who was to return as club professional in 1986 for three years before leaving to take up a teaching post in Germany. He was born in Cumbernauld and after his Helensburgh training he had spells as club pro at Irvine Bogside and West Kilbride before his appointment here.

Robert Farrell became the fifth club professional at Helensburgh in 1989 after spells at Clydebank Overtoun, Murrayfield, and Turnberry.

Born appropriately in Helensburgh he began playing golf at Clydebank at the age of 12, and then also at Windyhill, quickly reaching a high standard. When he turned professional aged 16 he had progressed to a handicap of one and had won the Dumbartonshire boys matchplay and strokeplay titles, the under-16 strokeplay and the club championship at Clydebank Overtoun, where he took up his first job which lasted two-and-a-half years under the guidance of Richard Bowman.

His apprenticeship continued with James Fisher at Murrayfield for three years, then for two years at Bob Jamieson's highly regarded stable at Turnberry where he was head assistant prior to his move to Helensburgh at the age of 23 along with his wife-to-be Vicki.

By this time, though still a very young man, he had already gathered a wealth of experience. This was not entirely in such matters as running a business, teaching, repairing clubs, and the multitude of other skills which a modern club professional must possess. He also had shown he could more than hold his own on the ultra-competitive Tartan Tour.

Robert Farrell: returned to the town of his birth to become professional in 1989.

In June, 1986, he equalled the record of 61, six under par, over Dalmahoy's West course to qualify for the last 16 of the Glenmuir Assistants' Championship, and the following April he was runner-up to Turnberry's Calum Innes in the Ryder Scottish Assistants' Championship at Hilton Park when it was a case of what might have been had he not opened with a 78. Scores of 69, 71 and 71 followed.

Although his playing opportunities at the time of writing are restricted, once this changes there is every chance of more success to come.

Two amateur players of note who have since turned professional are Martin Gray and Gary Orr, who have been leading lights on the Tartan Tour, Orr at the time of writing setting his sights on the more lucrative European Tour.

Gray was a junior member of Helensburgh for two

years when his parents, Jack and May, were clubmaster and stewardess in the late sixties.

Taught principally by his brother Gordon, the professional at Dumfries & County, Gray played his first golf at Bearsden and when he arrived at Helensburgh, attending Hermitage Academy for his final year at school, he was already playing beyond club level.

In that year, 1969, the two-handicapper won the Dumbartonshire and West of Scotland boys' championships and earned a boys' cap. In the Home Internationals he met Martin Foster who won by one hole, an ominous result because the pair were to clash again the following week over the same course in the final of the British Boys Championship. Gray came close but lost again, this time at the 37th where he was down for the first time in the match and, to complete an unfortunate weekend, the next day he played in the final of the Helensburgh club championship and was defeated by Peter Reece.

Martin Gray: his open highlight was playing alongside Jack Nicklaus in the 1986 Open Championship.
Picture courtesy of Jimmy Millar of The Herald.

Gray turned professional the following year and was an assistant to Derek Craik at Henley on Thames, then a playing assistant at Royal Wimbledon. He played the European Tour for two seasons with a best finish of 14th in the Carroll's Irish Open before back trouble put him out of action for a year. Thereafter, he took up the club job at Ardeer for 18 months before, in 1976, becoming the professional at Ladybank where he has been based since.

For 10 years from 1977 he was never out of the top five in the Tartan Tour order of merit, was a member of the British PGA Cup team on three occasions, and played in the Open Championship seven times. His Open highlight without question was at Turnberry in 1986 when he partnered Jack Nicklaus, then the US Masters champion, in the third round. Both shot 76s. Gray remembers his time at Helensburgh fondly and was delighted to have the chance to return in 1985 for the Catterson Classic Pro-am in which he shot a one over par 70 to be joint third.

Orr, meanwhile, promises to become the most successful professional with a Helensburgh connection, and in our centenary year even though his achievements thus far are already impressive you get the feeling that the story of this highly rated 25 year old might be only just beginning.

His potential was amply illustrated in the 1992 Bell's Scottish Open when, after opening rounds of 66 and 67 against the par of 70 on the King's Course at Gleneagles Hotel, he was right in contention and held his game together well over the final two rounds. A 71 in the third round dropped him back to six under par but he reached nine under par in the final round before stumbling a little over the closing holes to finish with another 71, good enough for joint 28th place and a cheque for £5,175.

This was playing against the cream of the European Tour and several top Americans. He finished just two behind Larry Mize, one adrift of Ben Crenshaw and two ahead of Seve Ballesteros. Such luminaries as Sam Torrance, Steven Richardson and Phil Mickelson did not even make the cut. That is the measure of his potential.

Orr was born in Helensburgh but his first golf was played over the Vale of Leven course where father Hamish was a member before joining Helensburgh when Gary was aged 10. The young Orr received group coaching from Brian Anderson, his handicap dropping from an initial 36 to scratch by the age of 18 by which time he had also been coached by Jim Farmer as part of the Scottish Youths squad.

His catalogue of successes included four junior club championships, the West of Scotland and Dumbartonshire Boys' strokeplay titles, and the 1984 Helensburgh Boys Open in the final of which he beat the now leading light on the Tartan Tour, Kenny Walker.

Orr was a boy and youth cap, in one match at Carnoustie teaming up with Andrew McQueen to defeat Ryder Cup player-to-be Steven Richardson and Andy Rogers on the final green at Carnoustie, and a member of the Great Britain and Ireland Youths team.

Orr originally went south when his father moved to a new job, but his extended stay had more to do with fate. Thinking of a club job in Scotland, he contacted Sandy Jones at the Scottish PGA to ask if he knew of anyone looking for an assistant. Gary was put in touch with Lee Johnson, who used to be at Powfoot, but was now at Burhill only half and hour from the centre of London. He completed his probationary period there in September, 1988, and for the following two years did not play a great deal, mainly working in the shop and giving lessons, but was then given freedom to play at every opportunity.

It was through teaching as much as anything else that he learned a great deal about the golf swing. Johnson was also helpful with commonsense advice which Orr put to good effect in practice, and Burhill's facilities in this respect are excellent. There are three big practice areas, one for professionals only.

Play was principally on the South Region tour and in 1991 Orr won his region's assistants championship at Beaconsfield, was fifth in the their professional championship at East Sussex National, and runner-up in the Mizuno Assistants Championship.

It was his sorties back north, however, which grabbed the attention, culminating in his victory at Renfrew in the Sunderland of Scotland Masters, one of the principal 72-hole Tartan Tour events. The success was not entirely a surprise as he had already announced his arrival in his first full playing season by finishing second in the Dunbar Professional Championship, third in the Scottish Assistants Match-play, and leading assistant in the Northern Open.

Hero worship: Severiano Ballesteros signs an autograph for young Gary Orr in the early 80s. Little could the swashbuckling Spaniard have suspected that his young admirer would finish two shots ahead of him some 10 years later in the 1992 Bell's Scottish Open.

Moment of glory: Gary Orr with the Sunderland of Scotland Masters trophy and there were some big names behind him in places two to five, Andrew Oldcorn, Jim Farmer, Paul Lawrie and Drew Elliot.
Picture by Andy Forman.

His performance at Gleneagles in 1992 was another step forward, and in November, 1992, he gained his European Tour card with eighteenth place in the final qualifying school at Montpellier. Then, having finished No.2 on the 1992 Tartan Tour order of merit, he was chosen for the three-man Scottish side to contest the European Teams Championship at La Manga along with Kenny Walker and Kevin Stables, the trio duly becoming European champions. Such is the pace of events that his story thus far could be a little out of date by the time the centenary book is published.

To find out what happened next - don't miss the bicentenary book!

The professional at Greenock, Graham Ross, learned his golf at Helensburgh where he took up the game at the age of 11 and played twice in Helensburgh's victorious junior McIntyre League team and twice in the senior side before turning professional at the age of 15 when his handicap was five.

Ross joined Cardross in 1981 when he was an assistant to Bob Josey, then took up the head assistant's job at Torquay under Martin Ruth, and was an assistant to Iain Parker at Prestwick St Nicholas before taking up the head professional's job at Greenock in 1989.

His playing achievements have included wins in the Ayrshire Winter Golf Association with a 69 at West Kilbride and another in the Devon Alliance with a 73 over the Jack Nicklaus-designed St Mellion Course, a score which at the time was the course record. On the Tartan Tour his best finish was 12th in the Under-25 Championship at Deer Park, Livingston, in 1988.

Although no Helensburgh member has come close to winning the Open Championship, one of our former juniors, Simon Holmes, has had a hand in creating one, namely Nick Faldo, who paid tribute to our man after his 1992 success at Muirfield. After leaving Helensburgh, Holmes had a spell in France before turning professional and joining the David Leadbetter stable in Florida and playing his part as a member of the Faldo backroom team.

Another protege of Holmes is the leading Swedish player Anders Forsbrand, further evidence, if any were needed by now, of the influence which Helensburgh Golf Club members have had on the game far beyond the town itself.

Graham Ross: turned professional at the age of 15.

CHAPTER 5

The amateurs

THE QUARRY: GATEWAY TO THE WORLD

HELENSBURGH can boast two winners of the Scottish Amateur Championship in J Morton "Morty" Dykes (1951) and Colin Dalgleish (1981), though Dykes, a resident of Helensburgh, did play under the banner of his original club Prestwick. Both were full internationals, Dalgleish going on to play in the Walker Cup, and Dykes, having already been a Walker Cup player, became a selector for the Great Britain and Ireland side.

Other members who have been capped at either youths or boys level are Gordon Dalgleish, Martin Gray, Gary Orr, Fraser McCathie and William Thornton, while Helensburgh teams have also excelled in the Evening Times Foursomes which they won three years in a row from 1978 and went on to be placed third on two occasions in the fore-runner to the European Club Championship, a record on which no other Scottish club has improved.

This chapter features those players who have performed with distinction beyond the club itself.

Colin Dalgleish with the Scottish Amateur Championship trophy in 1981.

"Morty" Dykes is presented with the Scottish Amateur Championship trophy at St Andrews in 1951. Picture courtesy of The Herald.

The swing of Colin Dalgleish was created at Helensburgh during the term of Brian Anderson as professional, and Brian, now director of golf and country club at Dalmahoy, was only too pleased to offer his assessment of a technique he played a large part in forming and which led to success in the Scottish Amateur Championship, a place in the Walker Cup team and tournament victories in America, Australia, Europe and Asia.

Overleaf, then, is Brian's analysis of the swing sequence taken by Andy Forman:

Brian Anderson.

A swing that went round the world

Picture 1. The set-up is characteristic of Colin's game; very orthodox and very solid. The club is aimed well with a good grip featuring a strong left hand.

Picture 2. Takeaway is indicative of the powerful nature of the backswing as there is a definite attempt to create width and promote a full shoulder turn. The head remains steady, with legs starting to move and hips beginning to turn.

Picture 3. The top of the backswing features the very full shoulder turn with club in a neutral position. The strong left hand grip dictates the cupped nature of the left wrist. The feet remain planted firmly on the ground, enhancing the wind-up and creating a storage of power.

Picture 4. The downswing is well under way with a good lateral shift as the need to drive through the ball is encouraged. The club is being led into the ball creating a good, late hit.

Picture 5. Through impact the head has remained steady, maintaining the feeling of being behind the ball and combining stability and mobility which creates the reliable technique so important during the heat of competition.

Picture 6. With the mobility of technique comes the positive follow through, displaying balance and control.

This is a good swing, well tried and tested, which will mature in a way that will not give health problems and continue to produce good results for many seasons.

Ten years on from Dalgleish's heyday his contemporaries in the 1980s read like a Who's Who of world golf. Among them are Spaniard Jose Maria Olazabal, with whom he halved a match in Paris, fellow Scots Colin Montgomerie and Gordon Brand Jr, Irishman Ronan Rafferty, Australian Craig Parry and leading Americans Jodie Mudd, John Cook and Joey Sindelar.

From the club point of view there is great pleasure in knowing that he learned his game at Helensburgh, where he still plays his golf, as an amateur and appropriately as an honorary member. In the club's centenary year he has been acknowledged as having a valuable contribution still to make to the game in his appointment as captain of the Scottish international team.

The Colin Dalgleish story began with his family

41 HELENSBURGH GOLF CLUB CENTENARY

moving in 1965 from Old Kilpatrick to East Abercromby Street just across the road from the Helensburgh club, when he was five years old. Four years later the family - father Douglas, mother May, Colin and brother Gordon, who is two years younger - joined the club en masse.

In the proper way of things they took lessons from the then professional Brian Anderson.

Colin and Gordon each started off with a cut-down mashie, and they were joined by John Harper on the practice area each Sunday morning. More clubs were added and they moved on to the course, playing the 15th, 16th and 17th, the 16th played from the side until they had the length to carry the quarry. It was a big occasion when Colin was the first to achieve this, and might be seen in hindsight as his gateway to the world. Then, after this nursery period, they left the nest and joined the junior section.

Brian recalls John, who tragically died in a car accident as a teenager, had a wonderful natural swing, Gordon's great flair and competitiveness and Colin's technical orthodoxy which, combined with a determined, dedicated approach and insatiable appetite for the game, identified him as a terrific prospect. Brian was never surprised at any of the successes which were to come.

Colin's first handicap was 31 and it fell to 22 by the age of 11 by which time he had won his first competition outside the club, the under-12 section of the Ayr Corporation Boys Tournament at Seafield. The prize, still etched on his mind, was two Penfold Commandos - balls very much at the lower end of the quality scale - but everyone has to start somewhere.

A year later his handicap was down to 12 and he achieved his first hole-in-one - from the ladies tee at the ninth using a No.5 iron - and at the age of 13 he was really beginning to blossom by winning the junior club championship, beating Kendal McWade, who was four years his senior and went on to become club professional at Eastwood, at the 39th hole in the final.

Three years later Colin was a boy international, had won the first of two Helensburgh Boys' Open titles, been a semi-finalist in the Scottish Boys' Championship, a scratch player and now senior Helensburgh champion.

In that 1977 Helensburgh final, having beaten Fraser McCathie in the semi-finals - and he was then to defeat him in the final three years in a row - he beat brother Gordon in a unique match. Seven years after taking up the game he was at the top of the club tree. World golf was next on the agenda.

That same year Colin was runner-up, like Martin Gray eight years before, in the British Boys' Championship at Downfield, where he learned a painful lesson having been two up with five to play against Ian Ford and ultimately losing.

There was, however, a first overseas success at East Aurora in Buffalo, USA, in the International Junior Masters and the following year Colin was captain of both the Scottish and British under-18 teams.

In 1978 he took up a golf scholarship at Ohio State University and although things did not work out ideally - he returned prematurely after two years - he stayed long enough to win the 72-hole Northern Inter-Collegiate Championship, ahead of runner-up John Cook, who came so agonisingly close to beating Nick Faldo in the 1992 Open Championship at Muirfield, and, among others, Joey Sindelar.

It is interesting to note that Cook by 1992 was already in the US top 50 of all-time career earnings with winnings of more than $3m.

In 1979 Colin was runner-up to Gordon Brand Jr in the British Youths Championship at Woodhall Spa, and a year later he won the Belgian Junior Championship in 1980 before returning home permanently to take up a place at Stirling University and becoming the first to merit a golf scholarship in Scotland, now an established practice.

That was in 1981 which was to be his big year. By reaching the quarter-finals of the Amateur Championship at St Andrews he secured his place in the Scottish team for the European Team Championship over the same course two weeks later, and although Scotland lost to England in the final, Colin's overall performance impressed the Walker Cup selectors sufficiently to pick him.

Successes later that year were icing on the cake, most notably the Scottish Amateur Championship at Western Gailes, on the Ayrshire coast.

He struggled through the early rounds, recovering from three down with five to play to win at the first extra hole against relative unknown Graham Pook in the second round.

That, apparently, was enough to jolt him into form and the scalps of former champions Gordon Murray and Iain Carslaw followed before defeating Allan Thomson by 7 and 6 in the 36-hole final before a crowd including a busload of delighted supporters from Helensburgh.

The Walker Cup teams at Cypress Point included for Great Britain and Ireland the now professionals Ronan Rafferty, Paul Way and Roger Chapman, and for America Jodie Mudd, Hal Sutton and Corey Pavin,

Colin meeting Mudd in the singles and losing by 7 and 5 despite being only one over par. He also lost to the little known Joey Rasset but there was a foursomes success in partnership with Duncan Evans, the former British Amateur champion from Wales, against Bob Lewis, still a prominent amateur, and Dick von Tacky.

Reaching the pinnacle of amateur golf was a huge achievement and there was more to come in 1981 when the Royal and Ancient club selected himself and the former British Boys and Youths champion, Malcolm Lewis, to compete in the East of India Open Amateur strokeplay and matchplay championships over Royal Calcutta.

Colin won the strokeplay title and was runner-up in the matchplay, beaten in the final by his team-mate before a gallery of around 500 on Christmas Day.

Success piled on success and the following year he was selected for the Great Britain and Ireland team to contest the St Andrews Trophy against Europe, he was runner-up for the second time in the British Youths, on this occasion to Welshman Philip Parkin, now a professional, and he captained the Scottish and British Youths side.

The Scottish team, which included Colin Montgomerie, succeeded in winning the European Youths Team Trophy in Paris, and it was in this competition that he earned his half against the then 16 year old Jose Maria Olazabal.

Early in 1983 he was encouraged by the university to compete in the Lake Macquarrie Open, unofficially the Australian open amateur championship, whose previous winners include Jack Newton, Bruce Devlin, and, the previous year Mark O'Meara.

In the field was Craig Parry, who was to become the 1991 Bell's Scottish Open champion, and despite being nine shots off the pace at the halfway stage, Colin compiled closing rounds of 70 and 71 against a par of 72 in near gale force conditions to win by a shot.

Later in the year he was first reserve for the Walker Cup match at Hoylake, but did not play. He did, however, win the Tennant Cup, the oldest amateur strokeplay competition in the world and played over two rounds each of Glasgow Gailes and Killermont, again winning by one shot after having been nine shots adrift at the halfway stage, closing with rounds of 65 and 66, the latter ending with a 40-foot putt on the home green.

He was also Scottish Universities champion that year, but just as quickly as the success story started, it stopped.

After graduating in May, 1984, he began his now successful business, PerryGolf, and although not consciously taking the decision to retire from competitive golf there never seemed enough time to work at his game and maintain it at the same high level.

The golden era was over, although he did remind his amateur rivals he could still be a force by winning the Tennant Cup again in 1988 and reaching the semi-finals of the Scottish Amateur at Lossiemouth in 1989, losing to the eventual winner Allan Thomson, whom he had beaten in that 1981 final.

Gordon, meanwhile, gained revenge for that 1977 club defeat with a semi-final victory over his brother (only to lose to Fraser McCathie in the final) before taking up a golf scholarship at William and Mary's College, Virginia, and after graduating worked for the American Junior Golf Association, of which he is now a board member, before becoming the American end of PerryGolf.

Though never quite scaling the heights of his brother, Gordon was in 1979 a member of the British Boys team which included Rafferty and Malcolm Mackenzie, now also a tournament professional.

After the 1981 Walker Cup, Colin was subject to some persuasion by Rafferty to turn professional like the Irishman was about to do and did seriously consider it, but he has no regrets about never taking this step, still believing he was not good enough, even though his record tends to suggest otherwise - remember he once beat John Cook into second place.

Neither might his story be finished. At the age of 32 in Helensburgh's centenary year there is still plenty time to attempt a comeback should he ever feel inclined, and in 1992 he was chosen to replace David Carrick as the Scottish international team captain, a responsibility which, because he was now required to attend major amateur events anyway, was likely to step up his playing career once more.

If the Colin Dalgleish success came at an early age, "Morty" Dykes's finest moment came towards the end of his golfing career when, just a few days before his 46th birthday, he won the Scottish Amateur Championship over St Andrews in 1951.

Although playing under the name of his original club, Prestwick, which was celebrating its centenary, and becoming the first member of that club to win the title, Dykes was also a member of Helensburgh, and lived in the town at Ardshealach. He had also won our club championship in 1948, in the final beating Ian Forsyth, now in his eighties and still a member. Ian recalls his opponent outdriving him often by 40 or 50 yards with prodigious hitting and being defeated over

36 holes by a margin of around 10 and 8, which was no disgrace given the calibre of his opponent.

The Dykes connection with Helensburgh was underlined in a radio interview on the evening of his Scottish Amateur success, during which he paid tribute to the help he had received from his friend Malcolm Grierson, then the professional at our club.

Dykes was beyond his heyday, having earned his first Scotland cap no fewer than 17 years previously, and was far from a favourite to win the 1951 title.

In those days there were two qualifying rounds of stroke-play, and he made the cut with three strokes to spare in joint 37th position after rounds of 79 and 78.

At the matchplay stage he beat T G McLeod (Douglas Park), J M Cannon (Irvine), and J R MacKay (Prestwick St Nicholas) to reach the final against J C Wilson (Cawder), who was 10 years younger and very much the likely lad to win.

Wilson led by one hole after the first round, having been three under fours and two up after 11 holes.

Wilson increased the lead to two after one hole of the second round, but it was reported that Dykes won the next two "with almost debonair carelessness."

Two more holes were exchanged out of the next eight and the turning point came at the 12th, where Wilson was eight feet from the hole in two and Dykes on the fringe, from where he holed a 20-foot putt. The Cawder man missed, and then lost two of the next three holes.

Dykes, now dormie three won the match one hole later after Wilson had to play out of a bunker backwards. The figures for Dykes' final 16 holes were:

| Out: 4 4 4 4 5 4 4 3 4 - 36 |
| In: 4 3 3 4 5 4 4 |

Two more pars would have given him a round of 71, which in those days was outstanding scoring.

Following this success Dykes was made an honorary member of the club at a dinner in the Shandon Hydro, attended by professional as well as amateur golfers. It was, by all accounts, an extremely jovial evening and not at all spoiled by the tough condition of the grouse on which the verdict of the diners was that it had been roaming the hills for too long.

Dykes, the Helensburgh representative on the Scottish Golf Union, was appointed a Walker Cup selector in 1956.

At club level the name of McCathie has loomed large in the last 20 years, Fraser and Lynn having won the men's and ladies' championships 16 times between them, Lynn a record ten times and Fraser six, just two behind Colin Dalgleish in 1992.

Fraser was born in Motherwell and Lynn in Canada, of Scottish parents, unlikely backgrounds for two of Helensburgh's most successful members, and even more so when you consider that they learned their golf in Yorkshire, Fraser at the nine-hole Thirsk and Northallerton club, and also at Oakdale, Harrogate, where Lynn was a member.

Swing of a champion: "Morty" Dykes in action at St Andrews.
Picture courtesy of The Herald.

Husband and wife double: Fraser and Lynn McCathie with the men's and women's championship trophies. They achieved this double three times in 1986, 1989 and 1990.

Fraser's job with an insurance firm brought the couple north in the 1970s, and they found Helensburgh an attractive place to set up home. Part of the attraction was because there was a good, friendly golf club on which they were to make an unprecedented impact.

Fraser, formerly a boy and youth international, became county champion and then led the club to three consecutive victories in the Evening Times Foursomes, once with Colin Sinclair and twice with Colin Dalgleish. These successes qualified them to play twice in the Kas Trophy, a competition for the champion clubs of European nations, at Santa Ponsa, Majorca, where they finished third on both occasions, the best finish by any Scottish club.

These performances are detailed below, but Fraser also had the rare distinction of playing in the Open Championship at Muirfield in 1980 as an amateur, an achievement marked by the Helensburgh club by the presentation to him of an engraved tankard.

Fraser and Lynn had decided to spend the week at the Open, based at Dewartown, 18 miles away, and then Fraser thought that as he was there anyway he might as well make a bold bid to qualify. Better to play than to watch and besides, it was a golfing area he knew well from his schooldays at Loretto.

His status as a scratch golfer allowed him in those days straight through to final qualifying, and he prepared for the daunting task in hand by shedding three stones on a steak and egg diet.

A 73 in the first round over Gullane No.2 held little hope of making it to the main event. In the second round, however, he was going well, helped by chipping in for a birdie at the twelfth, and was told that he was now in a position to qualify if only he could keep his game together. He promptly three-putted the next, but parred in for a 70 in windy conditions.

The wind then dropped and scoring by players still out on the course improved, ultimately leaving Fraser in a six-man play-off for four places. He secured one with a par at the first play-off hole.

On then to Muirfield and he found himself in the company of American Bill Rogers, whom he remembers as "an absolute gentleman", and another amateur, Nicholas Mitchell. Rogers at that time was the world matchplay champion and Open champion-to-be at Royal St George's the following year.

Nerves however, got the better of Fraser, who clearly recalls looking down the first fairway and seeing nothing other than a funnel of faces looking straight at him. Stage fright led to a series of shots missing the fairway and ending up behind the ropes.

He scored an opening round of 83 and improved to 76 second time round following receipt of a large card signed by well-wishers from Helensburgh, but missed the cut by 10 shots.

If Fraser did not play his best, mixing with the stars was still the experience of a lifetime, and as a measure of his two days in the big league he was asked to sign several hundred autograph books.

He also made a friend in Rogers, who, some time later at a tournament at Portmarnock, picked out Fraser from a crowd of spectators and came over to ask if he was playing that week. No he wasn't, but it was nice to be remembered.

Lynn, meantime, arrived at Helensburgh as a five-handicapper and reduced this mark to three, becoming a regular county player, and twice being a member of the victorious Dunbartonshire side, the high spot coming at Stranraer where she holed the winning putt in the final against East Lothian. Her opponent was the former Scottish Amateur champion, Lesley Hope.

Lynn never progressed beyond county play, but managed to keep her nose in front of Fraser in the club championship stakes, equalling the record of eight wins by Agnes Reece in 1990, and then creating a new record by winning in both of the following two years, a dominant run all the more remarkable for having cut down on play severely to raise two children.

Like Colin Dalgleish, the golfing story of the McCathies may not yet be over as they are both still young enough to resurrect their play beyond club level

Heady days: Fraser McCathie with clubmaster Gibby Beattie acting as caddie and Lynn McCathie as supporter-in-chief for the Open Championship campaign of 1980 at Muirfield.

should they ever feel inclined to try.

Helensburgh, meanwhile, reached the pinnacle of Scottish club golf in the years 1978-80 when the club won the Evening Times Foursomes, the national championship, for three seasons in a row.

The first success was at Prestwick, where Fraser McCathie and Colin Sinclair defeated Hilton Park's George Ellis and Bobby Millen by one hole in the final.

They had reached this stage by beating Greenock (2 and 1), West Kilbride (6 and 4), Fereneze (2 and 1) and Scottish Widows Fund (4 and 3). The West Kilbride team, incidentally, included Brian Gossman, the former rugby internationalist.

The final was unusual in that Fraser had been sharing accommodation with long-time friend George Ellis all week, only for them to become adversaries in the final in which Helensburgh were three up with seven to play.

They then lost three out of the next four holes, but won at the last when Bobby Millen missed a putt of less than two feet.

The triumph almost qualified Helensburgh to play in the Kas Trophy, a tournament among the champion clubs of European nations. It was to be played the following March but was switched to December which meant that if Helensburgh were to play they had to win the Scottish foursomes title again the following year at Hamilton.

As fate would have it, they reached the final to play Hilton Park for the second year in a row after having defeated Cochrane Castle in the semi-finals by 3 and 2. George Ellis was there again, this time partnered by Stewart Niven, while Fraser this time had teamed up with Colin Dalgleish.

The victory this time was more comfortable, though Helensburgh were only one up for much of the match, winning the 15th and 16th for a 3 and 2 success. And so it was on to Santa Ponsa, Majorca, in December, the three-man team being made up appropriately by Colin Sinclair.

Against 16 other nations, four rounds were to be played over the 7,000-yard, SSS 74 course, with the best two scores counting each day, a system which unfortunately for Colin Sinclair meant that in the event all four of his scores were discounted.

The team were to look back with regret at the first round in which McCathie and Dalgleish were going well only to drop a dozen strokes between them over the last six holes. Scores of 79 and 80 left them in 11th place.

In the second round Fraser had only 24 putts in a 74, and adding Colin Dalgleish's 77, this lifted them to 6th, and then to 3rd the next day with respective scores of 72 and 73. They finished in this position narrowly behind Rouen of France and Hamburg of Germany, and looking back to the tail end of the first round it was an agonising case of . . . if only.

Fraser ended the week in 6th place in the individual competition, and Colin Dalgleish 11th. The winner was Philippe Ploujoux, of France, and there's the measure of the standard of this competition. He went on to win the British Amateur Championship in 1981.

The point is that while Scottish talent was spread

A touch of tartan: The Helensburgh trio of Colin Dalgleish, Fraser McCathie and Gordon Dalgleish together with club representative Douglas Dalgleish in Majorca for the Kas Trophy of 1980.

far and wide among more than 400 clubs continental European nations, in those days particularly, had few clubs and those who represented their countries tended to be internationals or at least close to that standard.

In that light 3rd place was an outstanding performance. Helensburgh were to repeat that placing the following year and these are finishes which no other Scottish club since has bettered, although Kilmarnock Barassie came close in 1992 when they were fourth.

Helensburgh, represented again by McCathie and Dalgleish, won the Evening Times Foursomes for the third consecutive year at Dunblane, beating Pumpherston in the final, and so booking their place for the second time in Majorca, Colin Sinclair, who had moved to Forfar, this time being replaced by Gordon Dalgleish.

The same system operated, and this time all three players contributed scores over the four days. The aggregates of the two best scores on the opening three days being a steady 152, 157, and 155, leaving Helensburgh eight shots behind Ireland's Limerick going into the final day when the weather was dreadful.

Helensburgh came within one shot of the lead, but slipped back over the closing holes Fraser finishing with 79, Colin 80, and Gordon 81. The 159 aggregate left them on a total of 623, three behind Limerick and one adrift of Hamburg. So near yet so far, but on both occasions the team performed with distinction and put Helensburgh firmly on the golfing map of Europe.

The run came to an end in the Evening Times Foursomes the following year at Baberton where, according to eyewitnesses, McCathie was not at his best and spraying shots into a wide variety of bushes and heavy undergrowth giving Dalgleish a very hard time of it. Asked about the reason for defeat, McCathie is alleged to have said: "I thought Walker Cup players knew how to play these recovery shots."

Helensburgh's three national foursomes victories in a row is not, however, a record. Ayr Academy FP won four in a row from 1934 to 1937 when they were represented on each occasion by the same pair, J B Stevenson, an international player, and C J Louden. Stevenson went on to win on two more occasions playing for Troon Portland.

The qualifying route to the European Club Championship is now via area events and a Scottish final, using the two out of three scoring system. The Martel Cognac Scottish Club Championship final is scheduled to take place at Helensburgh in September 1993 as part of our centenary celebrations.

At county events, there have been a number of successes. The Individual Championship, known as the Wedgewood Trophy has been won by J Brash Jnr [1898], J Munro [1956], R McK Douglas [1965] and D W Weir [1974]. Today, this is a scratch 36-hole strokeplay tournament. Other well known winners include such famous names in amateur golf as Reid Jack, Frank Deighton and Charlie Green, an honorary member of Helensburgh since his Walker Cup captaincy.

The Wylie Trophy was first played at Helensburgh in 1897 and the best two aggregate scratch scores from participating clubs determine the winner. The number of players per club is typically limited to six. Helensburgh has won this historic trophy on seven occasions; T M Lunan / R L D Kidston [1907], E R Campbell / J Dingwall [1910], J Gilmour / S J Mackay [1923], I McDonald / I McK Still [1959], J Munro / E McGregor [1972], C R Dalgleish / R F B McCathie [1979] and R F B McCathie / I L B McCulloch [1981]. The County Matchplay Championship was won by R F B McCathie in 1977.

It is appropriate to include a brief reference to local League activity and other external golfing matters. The McIntyre League has been running for many years but we can boast of only one success in 1965, despite a few near misses. Bert Goodwin deserves a mention as the only match secretary to bring home this trophy but President Alan Christianson may well have a greater claim, as the Captain at that time. 1965 was also the year of the first major clubhouse alteration and the reader may wonder at the relevance of this, given that chapter 3 is about clubhouses. Let us just say that the club did not retain the trophy in 1966. Arriving at the league dinner, Evan McGregor and the late Douglas Lowe were asked for the said trophy. A U-turn was performed and the intrepid pair returned to Helensburgh, to find that this prestigious trophy was at best in a state of disrepair, having been removed from the cabinet during the house alterations. The official story was that the trophy was not available but in good hands. It is presumed that Gordon Hattle was successful in performing the necessary resurrection.

A more recent League within the McIntyre scene has the label of 5 to 8, meaning that handicaps must be 5 or more and those over 8 play off 8. Despite reaching at least two finals, Helensburgh has not yet won this event which comprises four fourballs, home and away, aggregate holes up deciding the winner.

Helensburgh were the first winners of the veterans competition which began in 1979 as a shadow version of the full McIntyre League. The veterans competition is restricted to those over 60 and no longer in full-time employment and those who regard play as entirely social are probably deceiving themselves. There is a keen competitive edge and although until the late 1980s it was sometimes a struggle to raise a team this is no longer the case and players are aware that they must perform if they are to keep their place in the team.

The league was instigated by Helensburgh member Paul Capel, who has since moved south and is a member at Lee-on-Solent, Hampshire. It first comprised Helensburgh, Cardross, Dumbarton, Vale of Leven, Clydebank & District and Clober, played home and away, but membership has since risen to 16 and each club now plays one another only once. The newcomers are Windyhill, Bearsden, Milngavie, Kirkintilloch, Hayston, Dullatur, Douglas Park, Hilton Park, Balmore and Lenzie.

The format is eight a side, comprised of four fourballs played according to handicap and each side has four reserves who also play although their results do not count.

Capel was followed as Helensburgh convener by Bill McArthur, Jimmy Miller and Denny Scougall and in the ensuing years the team won the McKinlay Trophy on two more occasions, once outright and the other shared with Cardross. Two players have been part of all three triumphs and they are Bill McArthur and George Raeside.

Helensburgh are scheduled to host the prize-giving dinner in 1993.

1979 Helensburgh	1986 Cardross
1980 Cardross	1987 Milngavie
1981 Vale of Leven/Cardross	1988 Cardross
1982 Vale of Leven	1989 Cardross
1983 Vale of Leven	1990 Cardross/Helensburgh
1984 Vale of Leven	1991 Helensburgh
1985 Kirkintilloch	1992 Cardross

The Thomson McCrone League was established in the 1970s, primarily to foster good relations between all clubs in Dunbartonshire. Known as The Friendly League, with handicap limits of 9-20, it was also designed to allow higher handicap players to play competitive golf over other courses. The present format is six sections of four clubs playing each other home and away, with the six winners and two best runners up proceeding to the knock out stages. Originally nine singles applied but a proposal from Helensburgh to change to five fourball matches was adopted in 1992. Helensburgh won at the first attempt, with team captain David Griffiths in charge, ably supported by a young Douglas Lowe and were beaten semi-finalists in 1991 and 1992. The related Forrest Trophy [teams of four from each club playing medal rounds] was also won over Campsie a few years ago, the competitors being Dave Loch, Dave Yorke, John Fraser and Frank Goodfellow.

The ladies, too, have had their successes and by 1959 Helensburgh were competing in the newly formed Allander League which is played on a handicap basis and designed to suit players with day-time commitments. Lack of success in the early days of this competition may have been due to the small number of playing members. In 1964 only 17 had handicaps whereas today the number is 71 out of the maximum membership of 130, the increase due in no small part to the group lessons initiated by professional Brian Anderson after his arrival in 1968.

As competition within the club increased, so did success in the league which Helensburgh won in 1973, 1975, 1977, 1978 and 1986. In the Harper Kennedy League, played on a scratch basis, Helensburgh were victorious in 1978, three years after the competition was inaugurated.

Helensburgh ladies who have been county team members are: Mrs Paterson (1909-1913 and 1920-1922), Mrs E Elderton (1912), Mrs Adam (1920-1926), Miss K Adam, Mrs Barrie, Miss M Bell and Miss D Herbert (early 30s and the last named two tending to play out of Cardross), and Mrs Lynn McCathie (1977-1980).

County champions have included: Miss M Bell (1934), Miss D Herbert (1935), Mrs R Adam (1936) and Miss K Adam (1938).

Helensburgh ladies have had a welter of successes beyond club or county level, most happening at Gleneagles. In 1972 Miss Hendry and Mrs Oppenheim won the Scottish Lady Veterans meeting; in 1976 and 1980 Mrs May Dalgleish won the LGU Silver Challenge Bowl and Gold Medal; in 1983 Mrs Fiona Fox qualified as a member of the victorious Scottish team at in the Ford competition at Lytham St Annes having won the Scottish Regional final at Gleneagles; in 1984 Mrs Lynn McCathie won the LGU Scratch Bowl; in 1987 Mrs Morag Carlaw won the Gold Brooch; in 1990 Mrs Katie Rogers was a member of the Scottish Rover Team which competed at La Manga having won a place in the Scottish final at Musselburgh.

In 1973 at a meeting in Dumbarton the McIntyre League agreed to inaugurate a league tournament for Juniors involving the same seven clubs which constituted the Senior League. Helensburgh won the first series, played in 1974 and were presented with the cup by the donor, Mr J Reid. They won again in 1978, 1979 and 1981 but have not won since although they twice have been runners-up recently.

TOM HALIBURTON MEMORIAL TROPHY

Tom Haliburton, one of Scotland's most successful and highly respected professionals, played much of his early golf at Shandon, Helensburgh, and Cardross and although he subsequently became an Anglo-Scot, based at Wentworth, he never forgot his roots. In 1975 he wrote to both Helensburgh and Cardross saying that he wished to present a trophy for an annual competition for junior boys of both clubs. Regrettably he died before fulfilling this wish but his widow, aware of his intentions, presented the trophy on his behalf.

In 1976 there was an attempt to make this the trophy for the Helensburgh Boys' Open, a move which brought a strong reply from Cardross pointing out that a national competition was not Haliburton's wish, and, besides, what possible advantage could there be to Cardross in such an arrangement. Helensburgh backed down.

The competition, which is limited to boys under 18, consists of a medal round over Cardross and another over Helensburgh and the trophy is awarded to the boy recording the lowest aggregate scratch score for the two rounds. The trophy is currently held by Joe Hughes from Cardross.

DAVID FULTON TROPHY

The David Fulton Trophy, presented by a former captain and president, is awarded to the boy under 18 who has the lowest aggregate net score for the two rounds of the Tom Haliburton Competition.

HELENSBURGH CENTENARY PUTTER

Despite the temptation to feature the centenary programme in its entirety in this book, such things are subject to detailed revision, so we refer only to one or two future events.

The idea of hosting a tournament for all Scottish clubs having centenaries in 1993 and probably for an unspecified number of future years, has come to fruition. The concept is an aggregate medal, based upon teams of three low handicap players plus three officials from each club, the latter's scores counting in a tie break situation. The trophy is a putter donated by Bill Cairns, which has been verified as being close to 100 years old or at least the blade is. For 1993, the acceptance is excellent comprising Baberton, Eastwood, Kirkudbright, Lothianburn, Northern Merchants of Edinburgh, Newtonmore, Pollok, Reay, Thornhill, West Kilbride and, of course, Helensburgh. Not least because of the large number of forthcoming centenaries, the interest of the Scottish Golf Union has been roused. It has been mooted that the SGU might take over this tournament in future years even before a blow has been struck.

BRITISH GIRLS CHAMPIONSHIP and BRITISH GIRLS HOME INTERNATIONAL MATCHES

One of the most prestigious achievements is attributed to the ladies, who have negotiated these major fixtures for our centenary. The events are scheduled for August 1993, with a practice match for the Scottish girls team against our own juniors in late March.

Hosting a major girls event is not a new experience because Helensburgh Ladies staged the British Girls Strokeplay competition on August 10-11, 1961, when the winner was Diane Robb of Wolverhampton, who had a hole-in-one at the 16th. The runner-up was Ann Irvine from Fleetwood.

CLIQUE OUTINGS AND VISITATIONS

A weekend outing to Callander in 1958. Back row (l to r): J Cummings, J Petrie, W Ralph, J Nicol, L McInnes. Second row: D Dods, J Maitland, D Ralph, L Waddell, R Rice, I Forsyth, J Spy, D McGittrick, W Fyfe. Third row: A MacKenzie, H Mercer, H Walsh, W Copeland, R Osborne, J O Smith, W Watt, J McIntyre, J Fraser, Mr Bethune. Lying: C Friel, W Forsyth.

There have been many outings of one day or weekend and even one week to various places and courses too numerous to mention although venues have included Callander, Royal Dornoch, Falmouth, Norfolk, Islay, Ireland, Isle of Man, Bournemouth, Florida, Spain, Portugal, France and even Dubai. We have been visited by teams from Las Vegas Golf and Country Club, Sharjah Wanderers and a team from the Far East, courtesy of Bernard McCreadie, who lives in Jakarta.

These excursions are invariably arranged by one or two enthusiasts, who naturally concern themselves with the invitation list. Even the president's men have their own annual game against Callander, organised by John Muir, and a new clique has formed recently called the 1991 Gowf Society, organised by Colin MacDonald and which played in its first year Kilmacolm, Balmore, Cathkin Braes and Pollok.

One of the most popular outings is for The Putter, originally presented and organised by Brian Anderson and Gibby Beattie. Beginning in 1980 at Blairgowrie, this competition is 36 hole Stableford.

In 1986 there was the normal departure by coach for Turnberry and distinguished golf writer Bob Ferrier was so moved by the goings on that he was compelled to write the following article, published in the March, 1987, edition of Golf World, tactfully without mentioning Helensburgh:

"It was the golf club's annual outing, normal procedure for many Scottish suburban clubs - the jaunt, one year to St Andrews, the next to Rosemount, and the next (if the club is well-connected and has a fixer) to Muirfield, the country citadel of the Honourable Company of Edinburgh Golfers and the Edinburgh establishment (just as the New Club on Princes Street is the town citadel).

As a new boy, member for less than a year, supporting the club seemed the thing to do. Besides, they leaned on me, saying they had 35 in the party for the 36-seater coach, and the fourball Stablefords needed "balancing". The call was for 6.30am at the club. We left at 6.40. By 6.45 the bar at the back of the coach was open - whisky, gin, brandy, vodka. At such an hour - hard men.

Before we crossed the Erskine Bridge came the pies. The pie, the round, hand-sized mutton pie, is a Scottish institution. Like all fast food, it is revolting and irresistible at the same time. In my youth it had been a tuppeny pie. Then it became a tanner pie. Now my research tells me it's 30p (six shillings!). At Scottish football matches, incidentally, its consort is Bovril.

Pies on this trip were compulsory - it was tradition, they said. Eat. Besides, the pieman, who had been awake most of the night making the things, was on the coach, one of the 36 - and a solid 5-handicap, by the way.

Turnberry meant coffee and biscuits, and more drams. It was a gorgeous, shimmering autumn day, one-sweater-warm, when Turnberry is the most beautiful place you could be and the West of Scotland is paradise.

The first round was on the Arran course, the Ailsa's little sister, but probably good enough to be in Scotland's top 50. I found myself with three sluggers who bombed everything 30 yards past me, not always straight. The one with the remorseless hook kept saying, "Ach, ah tugged the hoor" (whore).

On the back nine I found a swing, made it in 40 strokes to top the Stableford points table. Illusions of grandeur for the afternoon round set in. Lunch was a dense Scottish broth, mounds of sandwiches, and drams.

The afternoon round was to be on the Ailsa. In preparation, one fourball was seen to pack two bottles of Glenlivet in the golf bags. Two bottles came back, suitably empty.

Trolleys are forbidden on the Ailsa course. We had caddies. Your Turnberry caddies are usually old boys, creased by decades of beachcombing along the Girvan shore, courtesy of the state, who know every break on the green on both Turnberry courses. Archie and I were unlucky. We had young guys, friends, aged around 30.

I started the Ailsa 7, 7, 7. Listen, it's not hard to do. But could this be the course of the enchanted Nicklaus and Watson in 1977, of the preposterous Greg Norman who actually holed a birdie bunker shot on the third hole of the last round of an Open Championship, just two months ago.

Yes it could, and it was, and it is.

It had all gone. There was the lightning backswing - I kept thinking of the Sam Snead dictum, "Give me a man with a fat wallet and a fast backswing." There was the collapsed grip at the top, the round lurching heave with the right shoulder, the head up. Total, utter despair.

But as we moved along I realised what was wrong. It was the caddies, these damned caddies. They kept talking, that background conversation which you don't quite hear but you know is there. Come to think of it, they'd been talking as we teed off, at the first. It seemed to be about pubs and, of course, ladies. They talked when we were over putts and they hadn't a clue.

"Hit it on the right lip," they'd say, and when you did, it would break three inches - to the right!

When Colin yanked a yard putt of six feet on the ninth, that was enough. A four-handed explosion of language, none of it delicate, cured them. But it was too late. I did finish par, par, a gesture to the lovely condition of the courses, and maybe the caddies were just a straw to clutch at.

Ah, but there was high tea, a mountain of fry - bacon, eggs, sausage, mushroom, black pudding, with an escarpment of chips. Scottish portions are indecent. There was cake, and tea - and drams. There was the inquest hour, with drams. There was the prizegiving, with drams. We discovered the coach in the dregs of the gloaming, and set off.

Crossing Fenwick Moor, there was the on-coach video show of Langer's US Masters win, and a blue movie, they called it. It was traditional, they said, and compulsory - captive compulsory. The bar ran out of water. It was a minor irritation. The drams never ran out.

We stopped with a start, somewhere in the depths of Partick. All out. Why? "Fish suppers."

Fish and chips, like the pie, is an institution, equally revolting and irresistible. Soon the coach stank of fish, chips, salt, vinegar. It ejected me a couple of hundred yards from home.

Deep breathing was now compulsory. The sky was splattered with stars. I looked up and thought "Why me? Why me?"

But I expect I'll be back next year."

The winners, the ones who overcame more than the usual hazards of rough and bunkers, are:

1980 A Scott, Rosemount
1981 I L B McCulloch, Rosemount
1982 A Ralston, Rosemount
1983 J Cleland, Rosemount
1984 A Scott, Rosemount
1985 Pat Mundie, St Andrews
1986 J Belch, Turnberry
1987 D Carswell, Carnoustie
1988 D Carswell, Western Gailes
1989 C R Dalgleish, Royal Dornoch
1990 A Dunlop, Glasgow Gailes
1991 C R Dalgleish, Gullane
1992 A Dunlop, Prestwick

A 1992 aerial photograph of Helensburgh Golf Club and the town (above), while back down to earth (below) is the view a player has for his dreaded opening shot.

A tunnel of foliage, a daunting view of the shot demanded from the medal tee at the 2nd.

Two reasons to lift your head and admire the scenery: above the vista from the 5th green towards Ardmore Peninsula, and below from the 6th forward tee looking to the southern reaches of Loch Lomond.

Not a frequently admired view because we walk the other way, but turn round on your way down the 15th and admire the setting of the clubhouse against the Rosneath Peninsula and the hills of Argyll beyond.

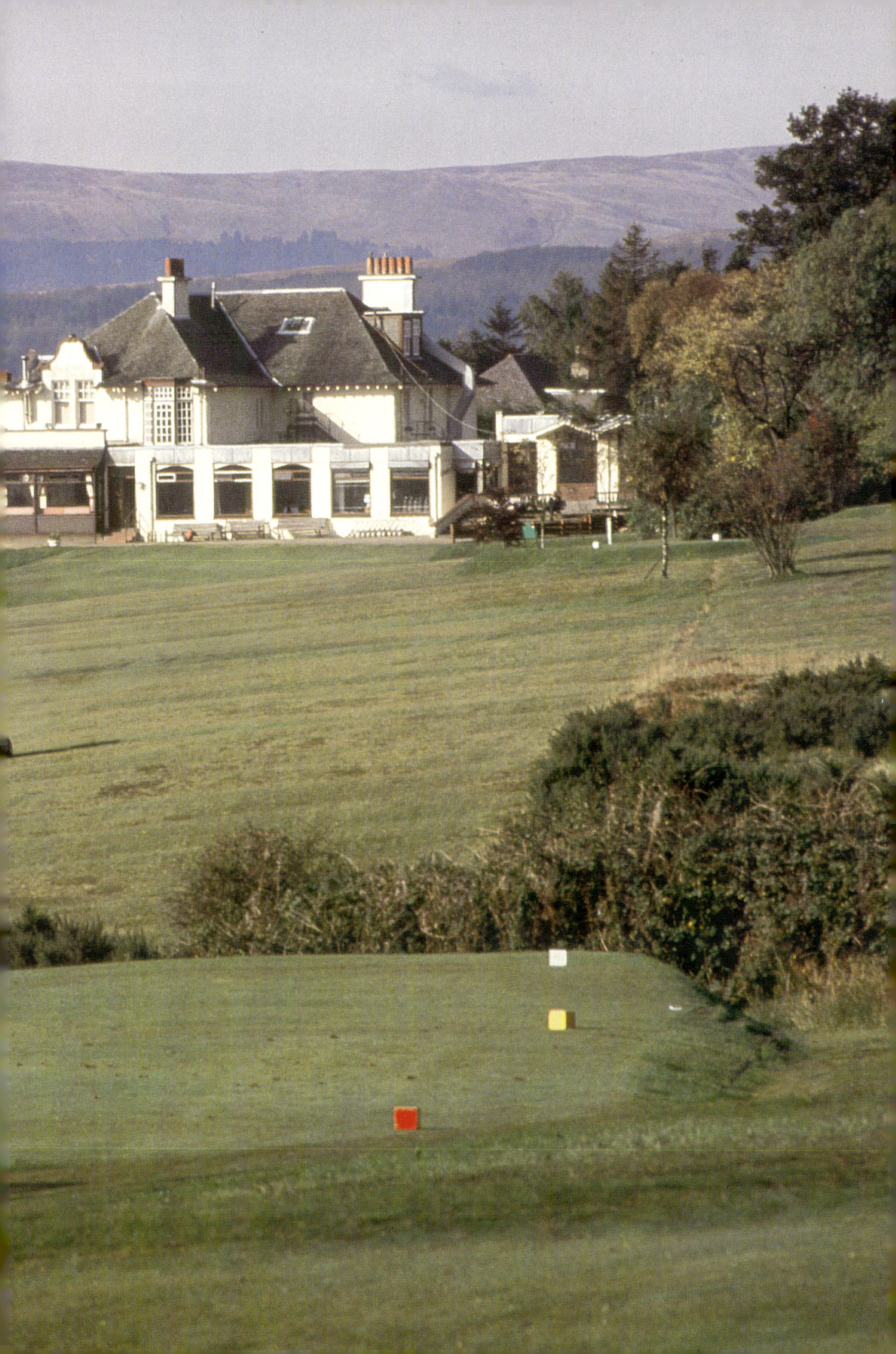

Off the straight and narrow, these are a couple of shots you could face. Topmost is the task in hand if you overshoot the first green and above, the shot required if your approach to the 12th finds itself in the trees to the left of the green.

The tree-surrounded 12th green, and below, the elevated 15th green.

The glint of silver (above) is the collection of Helensburgh Golf Club silverware paraded on the practice putting green while below is a familiar daily sight in summer at least, the veterans about to tee off.
The ritual caught here is the throwing up of the balls. How they land determines playing partners.

The pictures in this colour section, with the exception of those on the first page, were taken by Andy Forman.

CHAPTER 6

Pro tournaments and exhibition matches

WHEEDLING BIRDIES - AND BIRDS OUT OF TREES

PROBABLY the most prestigious match ever played at Helensburgh was on June 5, 1948, when Great Britain, represented by Irishman Fred Daly, and Welshman Dai Rees, played Australia, represented by Norman von Nida and Bill Shankland in a fourball match. This match certainly took place, unlike the laudable attempt of 1910 to entice Messrs. Braid, Taylor, Vardon and Herd, which seems to have failed for reasons unknown.

The British pair must have been favourites. Daly was the reigning Open Champion having won the previous year at Hoylake (he was also to be runner-up to Henry Cotton the following month at Muirfield), and Rees had twice been PGA Matchplay champion and was a Ryder Cup regular. However, the Australian pair won by 2 and 1.

The match, which attracted a large gallery, one of whom was struck on the head by a ball but was not badly hurt, raised £564 for the Scottish National Institute for War Blinded and St Dunstan's.

The biggest name fourball ever to play at Helensburgh were Fred Daly, Dai Rees, Norman von Nida and Bill Shankland (right).
Picture courtesy of The Herald.

Fred Daly (above), Norman Van Nida (above right) and Dai Rees (right). *Pictures courtesy of The Herald.*

Shankland, in fact, had helped bring in more than £150,000 for British charities by playing in exhibition games, and appears to have been a larger than life character. After play he conducted an auction of various items including the balls used in the match. It was reported that:

"Shankland was very enterprising and successful in his appeals ... he could have wheedled a bird out of a tree into his hat."

Wheedling birdies is a continuing Shankland family tradition, although Bill's relative, Kenny McDougall, still an active member at Helensburgh, used to beat them out of the ground as a keen game shooter of grouse and pheasant. It is an interesting family link. Kenny's wife, Marion, is a Shankland and her father, Thomas, was a cousin of Bill, who was born in Scotland before emigrating and his visit to Helensburgh was a golden opportunity to look up old friends and relatives. Family skills at golf continue in Helensburgh through Kenny and Marion's daughter, Fiona, an accomplished player, who is married to Alan Scott, holder of the course record of 64.

The match was played in dry conditions except for a shower as they played the last, but there was a high wind. A report in the Helensburgh and Gareloch Times said that spectators "admired the excellent technique of these great exponents of the game and the apparent ease with which they drove long distances and played their approach shots; it was only the players' putting lapses which gave solace to the ordinary golfer.

"Considering the perfect condition of the course and greens it was expected that a new record for the 18 holes would be put up, but the best score was Shankland's 71, von Nida taking 73. These figures make all the more creditable the score of 68 made by Mr J Morton Dykes in a match on Friday evening (the evening before). There was then little or no wind but rain fell steadily."

Shankland's scores were:
Out: 4 5 4 4 4 4 5 3 - 37
In: 5 3 3 5 4 4 2 4 4 - 34

Mr J K M Wylie acted as referee and Charlie Friel, W Forsyth, Kenny MacDougall and George Fraser acted as caddies.

Lack of local knowledge might have been a reason for the relatively high scoring and the story is still told that Charlie Friel handed Dai Rees a No.7 iron for his second shot to the 14th. Rees over-ruled this choice and insisted on taking a No.5 iron, whereupon he fired the ball over the green and on to the Old Luss Road. The Welshman turned to Friel and said: "I should have listened to you."

The next exhibition match at Helensburgh was three years later and two months after the Scottish Amateur success of "Morty" Dykes. The new champion was invited to partner professional Tom Haliburton, whose father stayed in Helensburgh, playing against Cawder's J C Wilson, the beaten finalist, and John Panton.

This match, in aid of the Professional Golfers' Association Benevolent Fund, was watched by a large crowd, and finished all square in good weather. The scores were: Dykes (37, 36) 73; Haliburton (33, 35) 68; Wilson (35, 38) 73; Panton (34, 34) 68.

The 68s were the lowest scores over the then recently altered course, but were not counted as official records unlike the 68s posted by Hamish Ballingall (Old Ranfurly) and Bill Watson (Whitecraigs) in the first professional tournament at Helensburgh, a West of Scotland Professional Golfers' Association 36-hole event in July, 1955.

Ballingall won the tournament, but only after an extensive play-off against Eric Brown (Buchanan Castle). This was over five holes, but the pair were still tied, each having missed putts of less than two feet. Ballingall won the next hole on a sudden-death basis, and took the prize of £25, the cup and £100 of unspecified extras. The leading scores were:

139 - J H Ballingall (Old Ranfurly) 71, 68; E C Brown (Buchanan Castle) 69, 70.
141 - B Watson (Whitecraigs) 73, 68.
146 - G Hall (unattached) 75, 71; W Rankin (Ranfurly Castle) 73, 73.
150 - T Dobson (East Renfrewshire) 74, 76.
151 - P Bullock (Glasgow) 74, 77.
Other score: 157 - M Grierson (Helensburgh) 81, 76.

The course record details were:

Ballingall
Out: 4 3 4 4 4 4 4 5 2 - 34
In: 5 3 4 5 5 3 2 3 4 - 34

Watson
Out: 4 4 3 4 4 4 4 4 3 - 34
In: 4 3 3 4 4 4 3 5 4 - 34

In 1969 there was another attempt to host an exhibition match, in aid of Cancer Relief. It did not then take place but was eventually organised for the summer of 1970. The match comprised Malcolm Gregson and Charlie Green versus Max Faulkner (yet another Open Champion to set foot here) and Jack Cannon, who had won the Scottish Amateur in 1969. The former pair won, Charlie Green being the most impressive player shooting 69 on a wet day.

Top professionals were to return for what was a unique pro-am in Scotland on Sunday, August 25, 1974. It featured, among others, the leading players in the British order of merit. This was just a few months before the breakaway from the British PGA of the European Tournament Players' Division, so effectively the top players in Europe descended on Helensburgh. It was the kind of pro-am which had never before been attempted and because the structure of professional golf has changed so much since, it could not possibly happen again.

The British PGA rules in 1974 insisted that the top 25 were invited and 12 accepted, among them Jack Newton from Australia, Ryder Cup captain-to-be Bernard Gallacher, South African Dale Hayes, and Irishman Eddie Polland. Others included Ryder Cup stars-to-be Sam Torrance, Jose-Maria Canizares and Brian Barnes (the last named tearing up his card at the first after hooking out of bounds), Australian Bob Shearer, and legendary Scots Eric Brown and John Panton, not forgetting, of course, Helensburgh's own Brian Anderson.

Newton, in fact, had agreed to play in the pro-am the previous winter, when he had partnered Brian Anderson during the Zambian Open at Mufilira, part of the then embryonic Safari Circuit, and Newton kept his promise.

The professionals had a high respect for the course, the best score among them two-under-par 67s by Bob Shearer and Irishman John O'Leary, who described the layout as "competitive." Only four out of 48 beat par and a further seven equalled it. Play was witnessed by a crowd of around 2,000, the largest gallery reserved for Bernard Gallacher.

They were, however, upstaged by the reigning Scottish Amateur champion, Gordon Murray of Fereneze, whose 65 counted for nothing other than a contribution to the joint second place team score and an unofficial course record.

The total prize fund was £5,000, quite considerable in those days, and there was some criticism from the professionals that the breakdown of this cash was top heavy. The joint winners received £800 each while those in joint fifth won less than £100 each.

That such a strong field could be gathered was due largely to timing, the pro-am being held immediately after the Double Diamond tournament, a predecessor of the Dunhill Cup, at Gleneagles, where some successful lobbying was done during the practice round by the trio of Brian Anderson, Jim Stark and Ronnie Jeffrey in a manner that would hardly be allowed today.

First to be asked was Irishman Christy O'Connor, and the trio approached him behind the professional's shop, almost pinning him to the wall. He said he would consider playing, but only on condition that in any publicity material his name was not suffixed by Senior. That other lad, his nephew, was Christy O'Connor Junior which was distinction enough. He was simply to be Christy O'Connor. As it turned out, however, he could not play because of a clashing event and his place was taken at a late stage by Canizares.

Next for the treatment was Doug Sanders, the American who missed that four-foot putt that would have won him the Open at St Andrews four years earlier. He was accosted on the first fairway and asked if he could play at Helensburgh on Sunday if he wasn't doing anything else.

Sanders told the intrepid trio to wait a second while he played his shot to the green, which he did successfully, and then told the Helensburgh contingent, quite pleasantly, that he would come for £2,000. That was his basic fee. "Well thanks but no thanks," was the gist of our representatives' response.

It was a case of if at first you don't succeed . . . Undaunted, they tried again and there was success on the 10th tee where Shearer was collared. Yes, he could play but only on condition that his two friends Stewart Ginn and Ian Stanley could come as well. This was more than acceptable, and in the end 50 professionals took part.

The star quality of the field duly bolstered, all the detailed preparation and last-minute opportunism almost went for nothing because of an overnight rainstorm. The first to be aware of this were Jim Stark, Douglas Dalgleish and Stan Chalmers who camped out in the drinks marquee beside the clubhouse to protect the contents from possible theft.

Around 3 am the so-called night watchmen were sound asleep on the job and had to be wakened forcibly by the driver of a catering van which had become bogged down on the course. Only two, however, were woken up. Stan slept through until dawn despite a drip from the roof saturating his sleeping bag.

It wasn't the only thing that was saturated; so was the course and an army of volunteers were out from 6.30 am with squeegees, towels, anything to mop up the greens and get the tournament under way which they did, an hour late.

The pro-am was hailed an outstanding success, not least for the Helensburgh club members who had the unique opportunity of playing with some of the world's leading players over their home course. And as the final adventure of the day, the club arranged for a police escort complete with out-riders to get Shearer to Glasgow Airport in time for a departing flight, otherwise the joint winner would not have been able to stay on for the prize-giving.

The tournament director that day, Tony Gray, is now the European Tour's director of external affairs and managing director of the new PGA European Seniors Tour.

Professionals' scores:

67 - R Shearer, J O'Leary (£800 each).
68 - A Brooks, T Horton (£350 each).
69 - J McTear, E Polland, R D B M Shade, D Vaughan, D Small, D Ingram, H Jackson (£90 each).
70 - A P Thomson, P Townsend, D Huish (£50 each).
71 - S Torrance, D Swaelens, P Wilcock, C de Foy, D Chillas, H Boyle, N Wood, I Stanley, J Newton, S Ginn, J-M Canizares, C O'Connor Jr, J Dorrestein (£45 each).

72 - F Rennie, W Milne, D Jagger, E Brown, W Humphreys, B Gallacher (£35 each).
73 - W Lockie, M Pinero, D Hayes, J Panton, D Webster (£30 each).
74 - B Anderson, R Walker, B Huggett (£27 each).
75 - R Wallace, J Noon R Carr (£25 each).
76 - J Anderson (£25).
77 - H Bannerman, P Touissaint (£25 each).
78 - J J Kinsella (£25).
NR - B Barnes, T Haliburton.
  Team scores (best net score at each hole):
59 - E Polland, D Carswell, W Goodall.
60 - D Chillas, G Murray, J F Nicol; J Panton, W Robertson, A S Harper.
61 - H Jackson, J M Harper, A Jeffrey.
62 - B Anderson, I Stewart, D Russell-Jones; W Milne, R D Graham, A D G Walker; R D B M Shade, A G Miller, W McRea; D Small, S Allan, E Boyle; R Shearer, A S Buchan, W Ross; I Stanley, I McDonald, A G Newing; S Ginn, I Donald, D H Davidson; C O'Connor Jr, I Morrison, R Smith.
63 - P Townsend, J S G Lennox, C Green; J O'Leary, I McCulloch, J D Baillie; E Brown, G Hyslop, P Capel; H Boyle, G Fraser Jr, W Rose; J-M Canizares, D S Roger, A Mauchline; J Dorrestein, W Fyfe, M R Niven.

Six years later, on July 8-10, 1980, the Coca Cola PGA tournament was staged at Helensburgh. There were some 100 competitors and the winner was current European Tour player Ross Drummond who beat the professional course record of 67 by two shots and equalled Fraser McCathie's then record of 65. In later rounds of the tournament John Chillas and Brian Marchbank each shots 65s as well.

The Helensburgh communications team headed by Douglas Dalgleish were widely praised for the efficiency of compiling hole-by-hole scores using walkie-talkies.

The leading scores were:
268 - R Drummond (Turnberry) 65, 70, 68, 65.
272 - B Marchbank (Gleneagles Hotel) 72, 65, 70, 65.
276 - J Farmer (Duddingston) 69, 69, 71, 67.
277 - J Chillas (Stirling) 73, 71, 68, 65; W Murray (unattached) 70, 66, 71, 70.

Only one pro-am has been held at Helensburgh since 1974, and that was the Catterson Classic on May 6, 1985, chiefly sponsored by mine host at the Ashton Bar, Gerald Catterson.

This event was an official part of the Tartan Tour and was attended by Peter Thomson, captain of the Scottish Region of the Professional Golfers' Association, and the secretary Sandy Jones, who has since gone on to become executive director of the PGA at their Belfry headquarters.

It is notable that Stephen McAllister, who was to go on to win two tournaments on the 1990 European Tour, was second on 69, one behind Ballater's Fraser Mann, the only player to beat par.

The weather that day was gentler than in 1974, and although there were showers in the morning, the afternoon was fine.

There was also a unique double in the team competition. David Carswell who had been victorious in 1974 in the company of Eddie Polland, was again in the winning group led by Dalmahoy's Ian Young, this time on a 15-under-par total of 54, which was pretty hot shooting.

The top scores were:
68 - F Mann, Ballater.
69 - S McAllister, Erskine.
70 - W Lockie, Kilmarnock Barassie; R Weir, Cowal; M Gray, Ladybank; K Stevely, Cawder.
71 - G Lennie, Clydebank & District; W Milne, Inchyra; J Farmer, Duddingston; I Young, Dalmahoy; G McKay, Glenbervie.
Others: 73 - N Colquhoun, Helensburgh. 74 - B Anderson, Helensburgh. 75 - C Elliott, Falkirk Tryst. 77 - N Cameron, Cardross.
  Team scores (best net score at each hole):
54 - I Young (Dalmahoy), D Carswell, C Smith, I Prentice.
56 - D Webster (Lundin Links), R Todd, A Ralston, D Gillies.
57 - K Stevely (Cawder), T Griffiths, R McDougall, J Taig.
58 - H Bannerman (Cruden Bay), S Barclay, B Traill, G Hanning.

There is one more Open Champion who has played at Helensburgh, namely Tom Weiskopf, having had two or three games in 1990, as a break from designing the Loch Lomond Golf Club's High Road course. That makes five Open Champion visitors so far, the others being Morris, Braid, Daly and Faulkner. Who is next?

CHAPTER 7

The officials

A HIGHER AUTHORITY THAN GOD, THE R&A . . . AND ON A PAR WITH ROYALTY

THERE is evidence over the years that the committee of Helensburgh Golf Club has had a fair conceit of its own importance, never more so than in March, 1910, when Mr. George Murray, the club's honorary secretary, wrote to the Secretary of State for Scotland, then based in Whitehall.

"I am directed by the Committee of Helensburgh Golf Club," wrote Mr. Murray, "to forward the enclosed resolution to you for transmission to His Majesty The King.

I have the honour to be, Sir, Your Obedient Servant."

What, then, was the cause for this momentous letter? It was, no less, the death of Edward VII and the beginning of the reign of George V. The resolution read:

"That the General Committee humbly express their sympathy with His Majesty the King and the Royal Family on the occasion of the lamented death of his late Majesty King Edward VII and humbly assure His Majesty of their loyal and dutiful allegiance on the occasion of His Majesty's accession to the Throne."

In 1992, a distance of 82 years, one wonders at the psychology of such a communication and what prompted it. We might imagine that the committee felt they did have a direct link with royalty through the Duke of Argyll, who was a member at the time, had opened the new clubhouse a year earlier, and who was married to Princess Louise, a grand-daughter of Queen Victoria. The couple lived at Rosneath Castle which was demolished in 1961 and became, less prestigiously, a caravan site.

They also must have been aware of the parliamentary rise of former committee member Bonar Law, who never reached the rarefied height of club captain, though he was on his way to becoming Prime Minister.

Such connections, despite professions of humility, may well have instilled a sense of grandeur which was further displayed in the 1930s when the club apparently abandoned the Rules of Golf as laid down by the Royal and Ancient Golf Club of St Andrews and introduced their own.

The Rules were by no means viewed as sacrosanct and the best example is the occasion when the members, by vote, decided that loss of distance was sufficient penalty for an out of bounds ball and that the loss of stroke as well, as decreed by the R & A, was too severe. This issue was voted upon on at least three occasions and may have had something to do with a view which exists today that missing the fairways at Helensburgh results in far more serious consequences than many other courses.

If this practice had continued then, who knows, Helensburgh could now have superseded the R & A as the ultimate authority on the Rules with a further significant advantage over the St Andrews - based club that we own our course.

It suggests that the committee and members of Helensburgh Golf Club were a law unto themselves, and four years earlier we might have some licence in suggesting that the committee, in introducing Sunday golf, were even above God.

Consider this leading article in the Helensburgh and Gareloch Times of August 11, 1926:

"Like a green bay tree the attempt to break in upon the sanctity of the First Day of the Week, by one hundred and fourteen members of our local golf club, is about to flourish. Sunday golf is to be introduced, and we have not heard the voice of a single clergyman in the town raised in protest against this Sabbath breaking . . .

Now that we have reached the stage when Sunday golf is to be considered right and proper, we may yet evolve farther along the same line. What about having the club house open and in full swing. Golf will be just as dry a game on Sunday as it is made out to be on any other day, and whether it be or not, can it be said to be sinful to take a small whisky or a glass of beer on Sunday?

When we get that seven days liberty, let us remember our brother who could never afford to play golf, but who can enjoy a neat dram. Let us be generous and do the job thoroughly, by opening the doors of the pub. Then there are those who would like a game of bowls or tennis, and others, who, not being the owners of a motor car, would prefer the railway company to arrange for their transport.

When we have turned the Sunday upside down in this manner, made it as we might say, out and out continental, then perhaps our pew-fillers will wake up and wonder why on earth they slept through all the row of such a change over.

Then we shall hear the trumpeting from all the street corners, heart-appealing calls for some prophet to come forth and assist in the melting down of the golden calf which was allowed to be set up, and which caused all this mischief.

Perhaps the powder of this sin will be cast upon the waters in the hope that all the haddocks, retired and otherwise, together with many other curious fish that have been eager to pollute the streams of our Scottish puritanism, will suffer the curses of their profane thoughts regarding Sunday observance.

Who is there in this country who believes that our days of labour should be increased from six to seven, and that is just what is going to be the lot of our working men, if we refuse now to nip in the bud these sleuth hound inroads upon the day of rest."

So there we have it: golf is to blame in Helensburgh for Sunday licensing, bowls, tennis and even trains. And we cannot say we were not warned. The seven-day licence finally arrived at the club in January 1959, more than 28 years after that dire prediction.

There was, in a sense, a moment of divine retribution when, in 1933, damage was done to the 2nd green by Sunday footballers and it was a regular occurrence thereafter on the day of rest for a police constable to be dispatched to patrol the course. The following year the club recruited a ranger, an ex-Glasgow policeman, to deal with trespassers.

That same year the committee had a problem in persuading Tom Turnbull to work on Sundays. The deal was that he would be present on Saturdays as well and instead have a weekday off with no additional remuneration. Turnbull eventually relented, but there is evidence he got his own back by persuading the committee to agree to a charge of 6d per quarter hour for use of the practice nets.

We might also mention that this hell, fire and brimstone leader came just two years after the Reverend Walker won the first club championship - presumably on a Saturday!

Another act of sacrilege has been perpetrated in recent years and that is altering the date of our National Bard's birthday. Rabbie Burns was born on January 25, but not as far as Helensburgh Golf Club is concerned. When our Burns Supper was inaugurated in 1979 it was decreed that it would be held on February 16 and there were very good reasons for so doing.

The best speakers were booked up for the proper night and so to have the best top-table cast the function was moved to the end of the Burns season, a practice which has been retained.

The caddies in the 1930s could have told us even more about our officials' visions of greatness. While sheep at this time were entitled to roam the course free, the committee directive about caddies was that they must exist in a pen beside the first tee and remain there until called for duty by the professional, Tom Turnbull.

Helensburgh Golf Club has, from the very beginning, been a family club with the result that the ladies' section is one of the oldest in Scotland. The ladies, however, have never been equal partners. They have always paid a reduced subscription, have never had voting rights in the overall running of the club, and have always had restricted access to the course and clubhouse in which a men-only bar still exists.

To the best of our knowledge no request has never been made formally to change matters and by and large the ladies appear to have been content over the years with their terms of membership. The co-existence has been happy and co-operative and recently there has been a small but increasing number of competitions involving both men and women.

The ladies share their centenary with that of the Ladies Golf Union which was also founded in 1893 and which the Helensburgh ladies joined in 1908, when they first played for official handicaps. That year also marks the beginning of the ladies' minutes books and was also when Lady Colquhoun was asked to become the ladies section president.

Although there was a junior section numbering 23 from the outset in 1893, it is not known whether that included girls who have competed over the years and in 1990 there was a total of eight taking part in the Strathclyde Junior League which had been established in an effort to stimulate interest.

The workings of the committee are often mysterious to the ordinary members. As is evident from the very first chapter, the captain and committee were appointed unanimously by acclaim at a public meeting.

One suspects, though, that the scene for these elections had been set elsewhere, probably in leather armchairs.

This is one assumed tradition which undoubtedly has been sustained. Clandestine conversations concerning successors continue to take place in various locations, and although connections with royalty and Westminster have not been kept the committee, certainly in recent years, has comprised a number of influential people in the local, Scottish and international business world.

As the earlier poetic correspondence has shown, the initial chosen few, despite their voluntary and well-intended efforts, did not all find favour.

So it remains today as the verbal pillory is wheeled out for the annual ceremony otherwise known as the Annual General meeting. Poetry certainly had more style, and other styles have changed over the years with a move, we suspect, from the autocratic to the democratic.

This, however, has had its drawbacks and one of the results is that the constitution and associated bye laws have changed from being very simple in the early days to the current rather long-winded version.

From 1954 to 1980 one of the great institutions of Helensburgh Golf Club was the Suggestions Book which documented gripes and groans which one suspects were sometimes written late at night after protracted discussions in the clubhouse in addition to the well thought out ideas it was intended to promote. Such a book existed in 1933 and there is a reference in the minutes to a suggestion to relocate the 18th green to its present position. The committee turned this one down but they changed their mind within a few years.

It appears to have been a useful means of communication among the members and their committees and many of the suggestions were in fact put into action. It is impossible to record them all and a selection, giving those with the qualities of humour and brevity preference, appears below and just to be safe all names have been omitted though the book remains in the club archives for any member who wishes to inspect it.

Regrettably abuse of the book caused its removal in 1980, and although thereafter it was available on request this is no longer the case. Having read through this tome 12 years on, it is respectfully suggested that the committee reinstate the Suggestions Book in 1993.

TOO MUCH SWEARING
July 1956: I suggest that something is done to correct the swearing that takes place in the clubhouse and on the course. I think I am justified in writing that that one hears enough of this sort of thing without paying six and a half pounds to hear it on the golf course.

Reply: The committee have agreed to take steps to rectify this complaint.

PURIFY THE AIR
November 1960: In view of the number of people using the lounge for cards, we would suggest that the committee consider the installation of an extractor fan to help purify the air.

Reply: This suggestion is being considered by the committee.

PLAY WITH THE JUNIORS
January 1961: In view of an encouraging number of junior members could not the committee consider a summer competition in which juniors and seniors might be partnered. This used to take place.

Reply: It is proposed to organise a competition of this nature in June.

AID FOR THE BLIND
June 1961: I suggest the erection of a marker pole behind the second green would be of benefit. The lack of this and a bell to indicate when players have left the green add considerably to the time taken to play this hole.

Reply: This matter is having consideration by the committee.

NO SCRATCH PRIZES
June 1962: Would the committee consider a small prize, say one ball, for the best scratch round in each of the monthly medals. This is widely done at other clubs and is an incentive to better play. Possibly a scratch sweep might attract reasonable entries too.

Reply: The committee is opposed to this suggestion.

DAMNED VISITORS

June 1963: Having played this forenoon in the Breingan Medal, it proved to be the most exasperating round I have experienced.

Due to several fourball matches - all visitors - my partner and I did not receive normal courtesies expected when playing medal rounds. We were even refused when we asked politely to play through. Surely visitors should not be allowed to play on medal days unless introduced by a member.

Reply: It is anticipated that restrictions will be imposed next season.

SORRY, TOO LATE

June 1963: We suggest to the committee that the clubmaster be instructed to view his catering responsibilities with a more pleasant and accommodating attitude. On arrival at the clubhouse on a stormy night we attempted to order four coffees at exactly two minutes past nine. We were met with the curt reply "You may not after nine o'clock."

Reply: The Suggestions Book must not be used for making personal complaints against any employee of the club. The committee therefore reject the above.

NO JACKET, NO ENTRY

July 1965: We the undersigned suggest that the compulsory wearing of jackets by male members within the men's lounge is unreasonable. We feel that any reasonable casual wear as long as it is respectable is permissible.

Reply: As a reasonable standard of dress in the club rooms is desirable no change in the existing rule is proposed.

BALL PIRATES

October 1965: Can something be done about "golf ball pirates" who roam our course, please? Today, from the eighth tee, I drove into the semi-rough. On reaching the spot I was asked by one of those individuals if I wanted to buy my own ball !!

Reply: It is not practical for the club to take effective action. Members themselves must warn suspicious "pirates".

GIMME A BEER - QUICK

February 1966: An improved version of the pump for draught beer please. One pint should equal 10 seconds flat into the glass. Signed thirsty Sassenachs . . . and one beer-slurping Scot.

Reply: Yes.

ETIQUETTE

June 1966: We suggest that a prominent sign be put at the first hole indicating the rules of golf etiquette and a reminder further round the course.

Reply: All members of this course are understood to know and observe the etiquette of golf.

TOILET DEMONSTRATION

July 1968: We feel that the state of the gents' toilet leaves much to be desired. There is a most unpleasant smell and it is suggested that the use of disinfectant would be beneficial.

The clubmaster replies: Today was as sultry as could be. The above members were at the tail of a long field. If they would care to ask the secretary he can tell them exactly how much is spent on disinfectant. The clubmaster will demonstrate how it is used.

Official reply: The committee are looking into possible solutions.

RUB OF THE GREEN

June 1970: On playing the 18th a hole, a high-handicap player is penalised if he pushes the ball out to the right and lands in a divot mark made by those practising. I feel this is unfair and there should be a free lift and drop.

Reply: This would be described as a rub of the green.

JACKPOT JUNIORS

July 1970: It has come to my notice that minors have been playing the fruit machines. I am certainly not a prude, but I do object when they win. I daresay if the committee looked into the Gaming and Betting laws they would realise the unfortunate consequences.

Reply: Notices will be printed and displayed prohibiting children from playing the gaming machines.

MISNOMER

September 1970: May I respectfully suggest that the committee change the name of this book to "Complaints Book".

Reply: One hopes for constructive suggestions.

POET'S CORNER

October 1971: We the undersigned would respectfully suggest that a sad lack of social activity in the club could be remedied this year if a Burns Supper could be organised.

Reply: This has been passed to the social convener for serious consideration.

A CLEAN WIPE
December 1971: May I suggest that we provide tissue type toilet paper for the use of members.

Reply: This is a marginal request but some attempt will be made to satisfy.

PROTECT CHILDREN - AND BALLS
August 1972: The general opinion of players is that a suitable fence should be erected to stop children playing on and beyond the 15th and 16th greens. It is obvious that, apart from theft, there is the much more serious question of children who cannot always be observed in this area getting struck and seriously injured in the firing line.

Reply: We are again pursuing very strongly with the Ministry of Defence the vandalism and nuisance of children from the Churchill Estate. We are hoping to convince them that the fence should be continued round the 16th tee.

NOT TOO SQUARE
January 1973: Are we too "square" to suggest jackets in the mixed lounge?

Reply: No you are not. The committee will take action on this.

WE WANT BIG BROTHER (1)
June 1974: I wish to point out that slow play is now becoming so bad that something must now be done if the medals are not going to grind to a halt. It must now be time for the committee to ask members to act as marshals on medal days.

Reply: This matter is under review but the committee doubt whether sufficient members could spare the time to act as marshals on a regular basis.

MAGNETIC POOL
February 1976: Being anything other than a killjoy and I believe a very ordinary member, I have observed with some degree of concern the "magnetic" appeal of the pool table upon our very promising junior members. Can I request our committee to give a clear ruling on the use of this amenity.

Reply: The committee have decided that junior members are not permitted in the pool/card room under any circumstance.

TOO DEAR AT 75P
September 1976: May I respectfully request that the committee reconsider the 75p charge for members' guests. In my opinion this is a gross over-charge.

Reply: The committee have agreed to reduce all guests of members to 50p.

WE WANT BIG BROTHER (2)
February 1977: I suggest that the committee should arrange to have the telescope reassembled and mounted upstairs where members would be able to observe play in medals and competitions at the furthermost points of the course. (Possibly handy also for members to observe slow play).

Reply: Telescope is already being repaired and reassembled. Where do you intend to site it? It was in the junior room.

SKIRTING ROUND A PROBLEM
March 1977: As a full member of this golf course I take grave exception to being barred from the mixed lounge because I did not bring a jacket. I make the suggestion that the question of dress should apply also to the ladies and the juniors where golf apparel should not be worn in the lounge. I shall wear a jacket when ladies wear dresses.

Reply: The committee's considered opinion is that the majority of members are satisfied with the rule as it stands.

COLD LIGHT OF DAY
December 31, 1977 (presumably late at night): I suggest that the incumbent committee resign en masse.

January 2, 1978 (presumably early in the morning): I withdraw the preceding without reservation and offer my apology to my committee.

MOVABLE TEES
January 1978: I suggest that in windy weather the tee at the 2nd hole be moved forward and the one at the 10th backwards or vice versa depending on the direction of the wind. This would enable the average hitter to get up in two at both holes (in medal rounds).

Reply: This is not practical.

CHALLENGE TO THE ENGLISH
May 1978: I note that there is an ever increasing English contingent in HGC. Would it perhaps be a good idea to have an annual England v Scotland match (at golf I mean). I feel that the English would offer strong opposition especially since they are not represented this year in the world cup.

Reply: If the subscribers are prepared to organise such a match the necessary facilities would be made available.

BODY OF OPINION

May 5, 1979: Smell in the entrance hall is getting a bit overpowering.

May 14, 1979: The body in the hall now appears to be decomposing.

May 15, 1979: Ressurecit Sicut Dixit.

May 20, 1979: Bless you, father!!

Reply: Remarks above noted.

LOST AND FOUND

May 1980: It is now over three years since my suggestion that the telescope be repaired and used in the club. Has it been repaired?

Reply: Despite inquiries the telescope cannot be traced.

Footnote 1992: While searching for minutes books for this centenary volume the telescope was found in the loft above the junior room.

NO IDLE THREAT

January 1980: Gentlemen, a very few members continue to abuse this Suggestions Book. The latest abuse is the removal of pages 186-189 inclusive. Should this continue, the committee will have little choice but to remove the book, amending bylaw 22 as necessary.

Footnote: A further abuse on page 193 in September of the same year caused this threat to be carried out.

One disappointment from our far-from-complete records is to discover that at one time there was a captain's photo gallery which was later abandoned when one captain argued for a Captain's Board instead. Since then the entire gallery for the first forty years or so has disappeared, when it had been the practice for the outgoing captain to donate one of himself. The gallery has been re-instated but many faces are missing.

Listed in this chapter are the presidents, captains, secretaries, lady captains and honorary presidents. The last category have rarely, if ever, played an active part in the club although Sir Ivar Colquhoun was persuaded to sell us some of his land. His predecessors were Sir James, Sir Alan J and Sir Iain, Sir Ivar being honorary president since 1948.

Many Helensburgh ladies have been members of the Dumbarton and Argyll Ladies Golf Association and in 1992 there were 26 full members. The first county meeting was on January 28, 1909, when Mrs Edith Paterson of Helensburgh was elected first captain and was on the committee until she resigned in 1924, having also been a player most of the time. During the first year of the association, the county played a match against Lanarkshire at Helensburgh on May 4. Other Helensburgh ladies who have been county captains are Mrs E Elderton in the 1920s, Mrs Porteous in the 1930s and Miss Bell from 1937-1947, becoming president for 17 years from 1971. She first played in the county team in 1928.

Mrs Agnes Reece was on committee in 1969 and for many years since then Helensburgh have had a representative.

The men, too, have been represented on the county executive, J G Ure and Douglas Dalgleish as president, Robert Stanton as secretary, and R R Herbertson and Jim Stark on committee.

PRESIDENTS

If the committee can be compared to the House of Commons, then the role of president is head of the House of Lords, a body perhaps comprising past captains. There are no rules concerning the choice of president, though in the recent past he is the former captain willing to accept the position whose term of office is the oldest. His role is unspecified, though it is more than just a charismatic figurehead.

Ideally his unconstituted authority is determined by the respect, invariably high, with which he is held in the club. This was put into effect within the last five years when the current president, Alan Christianson, chaired a meeting of past captains to discuss the way forward for the club, in particular to discuss the plan to sell the lower half of the course, and earlier, David Fulton as president had been invited to attend a committee discussion on the constitution.

There is a view that the president should be asked to perform a specific function such as preside over regular meetings of this kind with the aim of taking stock and looking at the club in the wider context, perhaps prior to the annual past captains' dinner.

The introduction in 1992 of the president's chair in the men's lounge has provided a talking point not least in the question of protocol as to whether an ordinary member should sit in this chair when the president is not there.

Like the nature of presidency, there is no definitive answer to this except to observe that after the initial curiosity when most people had a "shot" amid gentle banter the tendency has been to leave it vacant, probably out of respect.

What it has certainly achieved is a heightened awareness both of the position of president and the person who holds it, which is as it should be.

The list below is as complete as we can make it, though because of the absence of long sections of our records there are uncertainties over precise dates and in some instances the members so honoured. For example, the inclusion of Alexander Breingan is an educated guess. We find it hard to imagine he was not a president. Sadly we also record that a few vice presidents passed away before attaining the honour.

1893-94 R Kidston	1931-40 D J Young
1894-00 J Mitchell	1940-46 J D Bonnar
1900-02 A Breingan	1946-54 R R Herbertson
1902-18 W Middleton Campbell	1954-63 J Miller
1918-27 J G Ure	1963-83 D Fulton
1927-28 W H Kidston	1983-85 A G Miller
1928-31 W T MacLellan	1985 - A Christianson

CAPTAINS

While the president is chosen, the captain is elected. This process takes place at the Annual General Meeting, and even though the incumbent's choice as vice-captain appears to follow automatically this is not a foregone conclusion. The final decision rests with the voting members. The majority of captains serve two years, though some have settled for one and others longer.

His - and as matters stand it is not possible for a lady member to become captain - task is to ensure that the committee of management run the club's affairs to the satisfaction of the majority of voting members. The constitution provides the operational framework but the captain, who chairs the AGM, is also expected to propose amendments, especially in response to changing external circumstances like alterations in the law. In the event of dissension the buck stops with the captain.

While these matters are fairly clearly defined, it can also be said that a captain has a wide scope to make of his term of office what he may. In living memory, and almost certainly beyond, a captain has added his personality to the task. That is probably more important than anything as social skills are called upon weekly, if not daily, to be available to chat and joke with members and guests alike as well as listen to grievances and help keep the mood of the club bright, light and convivial.

The captain is called upon to speak on occasions such as the annual prize-giving, the conclusion of inter-club matches - when it helps if he has also been on the course as the No.1 supporter - and sundry other occasions. In short, it is a demanding and time-consuming job.

Mention has been made of a move over the first 100 years from the autocratic to the democratic, but for the position to remain tenable a degree of autocracy must be retained in day-to-day running. The captain is in charge, and instances frequently arise when decisions must be made on the spot because they cannot wait for the monthly committee meeting. His judgment is also called upon as to whether or not a matter can wait. Committee members ultimately support him in such cases. The course purchase was a good example.

Those who have held this post will tell you, virtually to a man, that as their term has unfolded they increasingly look forward to being a past captain.

1893-94 Alexander Breingan	1947-49 J K M Wylie
1894-96 W H Kidston	1949-51 Alex Hart
1896-97 John W Spence	1951-52 Murray Purvis
1897-98 John G Ure	1952-53 A J McIntosh
1898-99 Lewis H Smith	1953-54 G A Workman
1899-01 R M Wilson	1954-55 A G Miller
1901-05 A M M G Kidston	1955-56 J Campbell
1905-07 George R Fleming	1956-57 J McIlraith
1907-10 Walter T Maclellan	1957-59 W Aitkenhead
1910-12 C A Nicholl	1959-60 H J Weir
1912-14 David J Young	1960-62 F D Little
1914-17 C T Reid	1962-63 J G Lennox
1917-19 R O Elderton	1965-67 J P Orr Erskine
1919-21 J D Bonnar	1967-69 L P Bamford
1921-23 J Russell Martin	1969-70 D B Lowe
1923-25 G H Paterson	1970-72 John Baillie
1925-26 J J Haining	1972-74 G Leaf
1926-28 R R Herbertson	1974-76 I L B McCulloch
1928-30 W K MacLachlan	1976-77 M Kirk
1930-32 R T Templeton	1977-79 J Stark
1932-34 James Miller	1979-81 D S Dalgleish
1934-36 George Fairbairn	1981-83 P K Mill
1936-38 A D Downes	1983-85 R G Hattle
1938-40 K W Warden	1985-87 I G Plenderleath
1940-42 John Bruce	1987-89 J D Steele
1942-44 Douglas H Taylor	1989-91 J S Craig
1944-47 David Fulton	1991- T J Inglis

LADY CAPTAINS

As stated elsewhere, there have been Lady golfers at Helensburgh since 1893 and by 1905 a formal Ladies Section was in place. The Ladies Section has its own Annual General Meeting in November. The Lady Captain is elected for a term of office of two years. Recent thoughts concerning a term of one year only have been abandoned, for the time being at least.

The Lady Captain works with a committee of nine ladies, including vice captain, secretary, treasurer, handicap secretary and match secretary. Together they are responsible for the organisation of all LGU weekly competitions, matches in the Harper Kennedy and Allander leagues, plus several mixed events involving gents and juniors. The section runs its own finances and at the end of each year is in a position to contribute to various charities.

Nowadays, the lady captain and vice captain have access to the monthly meetings of the general committee, though this is not entirely new as in 1964 the lady captain was invited to assist in the interview of the new steward. This is a great help to the ladies section and a popular innovation, envied by other clubs without this facility.

As the table reveals, several ladies have served more than one term of two years.

1905-07 Mrs Snell Anderson	1960-61 Mrs B E Porteous
1907-09 Mrs J Paterson	1961-62 Mrs A G Miller
1909-11 Miss C M Gardner	1962-63 Mrs A Reece
1911-13 Miss A A Lamont	1963-64 Mrs M K Lennie
1913-14 Mrs E A Brown	1964-65 Mrs J Burt
1914-19 Mrs H Bell	1965-66 Mrs J M Ferrie
1919-21 Mrs A N Paterson	1966-67 Miss J R Rankin
1921-23 Mrs E M Elderton	1967-69 Mrs A Reece
1923-25 Mrs B Paterson	1969-71 Mrs A G Miller
1925-26 Mrs Crabbe	1971-73 Miss M E Bell
1926-31 Miss F S MacPhee	1973-75 Mrs F Gilchrist
1931-34 Miss J R Young	1975-79 Mrs J Ramsay
1934-36 Miss M J Connell	1979-81 Mrs E Fairlie
1936-38 Mrs E G Barrie	1981-82 Mrs V McIntyre
1938-47 Miss H Young	1982-83 Mrs E Shepherd
1947-49 Mrs M Thomson	1983-85 Dr K E Belch
1949-52 Miss M E Bell	1985-87 Mrs A Prime
1952-54 Mrs B E Porteous	1987-89 Mrs A Johnstone
1954-57 Miss E E Stanton	1989-91 Mrs A Halligan
1957-59 Miss G M Gibson	1991- Mrs M Dalgleish
1959-60 Miss J R Rankin	

JUNIOR CAPTAINS

1978 J M Graham	1986 C J Reid
1979 J M Graham	1987 C J Reid
1980 E D McLean	1988 C F Woess
1981 B R Mill	1989 P A Mundie
1982 T A D Reid	1990 N Fortune
1983 A D Fraser	1991 M Currie
1984 J E Graham	1992 L Latham
1985 K D Reid	

SECRETARIES

The early secretaries were viewed as important, if only by themselves and yet this is how it should be. Some of the most useful sources of information about the club have been the early handbooks, which have yielded various facts about layout, competitions and so on but the secretaries of the day ensured, most of all, that their own terms of office were recorded for posterity. At various times the secretary doubled up as treasurer but we do not record these here.

1893-95 W Lunan and	1932-35 G C Forbes
J M Murray	1935-42 R Stanton
1895-98 H H Ormond	1942-63 W G Clements
1898-00 A MacGregor	1963-66 S F Graham
1900-01 A Laurie	1966-75 J A McAuley
1901-16 H H Ormond	1975-77 F D Little
[assisted by G R Murray	1977-79 K Angus
in HHO's absence]	1979-84 R D Phoenix
1916-26 R Stanton	1984-87 R C McKechnie
1926-32 J R Martin	1987- Mrs A C McEwan

Featuring our active office bearers does not do justice to all who have served the club, which means the members, over 100 years. There are many who have undertaken important and time-consuming tasks, provided materials and artifacts, the details of which are hidden from sight.

There is no way of knowing of, let alone recording these various endeavours in any complete sense. One can only pay anonymous tribute to all concerned except perhaps light-hearted mention of two who are currently active, Jimmy Nicholson and Gordie Lennox.

Jimmy has established a new career as starter and general aide to the match and handicap secretary, especially on competition days. His reputation as official, or should we say officious, starter has spread beyond Helensburgh - the Dumbartonshire Golf Union know not to bring their own. One downside, however, has been the marked increase in the Tippex order, but budgets have been adjusted to ensure that supplies are maintained.

Gordie, a past captain, is currently 88 and is a known menace on the golf course. When the weather is clement he steadfastly plays a few holes using a variety of cross-country routes. His main claim to fame has been his extraordinary ability to appear out of the bushes at crucial moments and totally distract players. On one occasion Geordie said: "You shouldn't be putting when I am talking."

Ronald R Herbertson: a sportsman and diplomat. He was club champion, captain and president and he was also provost of Helensburgh.

There are some interesting cases, early and late, of members having made outstanding contributions to life outside the club. Former town Provosts Alexander Breingan (1863-69) and Ronald R Herbertson (1927-30) are worthy of note in this context and more would have been written about them had we been able to uncover more details as are other former Provosts, J Mitchell (1890-93), A M M G Kidston (1911-12), J D Bonnar (1912-18), and J Russell Martin (1936-41), all of whom were either club presidents, captains, or both.

We are able, though, to write at length about Andrew Bonar Law and Douglas Dalgleish.

ANDREW BONAR LAW

"A man without vanity"

Andrew Bonar Law: the Helensburgh Golf Club member whose address was 10 Downing Street, London. Picture courtesy of The Herald.

A profile of Bonar Law (1858-1923) is included not so much for his contribution to Helensburgh Golf Club, though he was a member of the first committee in 1893 at the age of 35. It is because he went on to become Prime Minister in 1922, albeit for just 209 days. Never let it be said that serving on our committee does not have possibilities for the ambitious.

The club, in fact, has in its possession a membership list from 1922 including Bonar Law with his address as 10 Downing Street, London, though by that time it must be said that his visits to Helensburgh were infrequent if ever at all.

He was the first man of colonial birth to become Prime Minister, having been born in New Brunswick, Canada. His father, the Reverend James Law, was a Presbyterian minister and an Ulsterman with a farming background, and the Helensburgh connection was via his mother, Elizabeth, daughter of William Kidston, an iron merchant whose business was in Glasgow. Bonar Law was the youngest of four sons.

The manse was a remote farmhouse near the mouth of the Richibucto river and the congregation largely settlers from Dumfries and Galloway. Bonar Law's mother died when he was two years old, and he was brought to Helensburgh by an aunt at the age of 12, his father, by all accounts, an increasingly melancholy man.

From his simple home, Bonar Law was now in affluent surroundings, but his humble background had already shaped his personality. He was considered a man without vanity, and the influence of his father was not lost either as he was to become a staunch supporter of the loyalist minority in Ireland.

Bonar Law could also be regarded as a late developer. He attended Glasgow High School and Glasgow University, never showing unusual promise. His relatives, William, Richard and Charles Kidston were partners in a Glasgow firm of merchant bankers mainly involved in financing trade in iron and steel, and he joined this firm which later was merged in the Clydesdale Bank, of which Bonar Law became a director.

The beginnings of his political career can be traced to his involvement in the Glasgow Parliamentary Debating Association, where he made himself familiar with parliamentary procedure and impressed officials of the Conservative and Liberal Unionist Association, who adopted him as their candidate for Blackfriars and Hutchesontown in 1900. He was duly elected and became an MP at the age of 42.

In Helensburgh he had met and married Annie Pitcairn, by whom he had four sons and two daughters.

She died in 1909, and after that it would seem his local connection weakened as he immersed himself in politics.

By that time, however, he had already made his mark at Westminster even though his maiden speech was largely ignored because on the same day none other than Winston Churchill was also making his maiden speech. However, there were more speeches to come, and so impressive were they that after 18 months he was appointed parliamentary secretary to the Board of Trade.

He lost his seat at Blackfriars, but was re-elected at Dulwich and then Bootle, Lancashire. His main election issues of those times, interestingly, were naval supremacy and not merely superiority over Germany, the defence of the loyal minority in Ireland against the imposition of a tyranny, and tariff reform as the greatest of all social reforms.

He succeeded Balfour in 1911 as Unionist leader in the House of Commons, was colonial secretary in 1915-16, then a member of the War Cabinet, Chancellor of the Exchequer from 1916-18, Lord Privy Seal in 1919 by which time he was MP for Central Glasgow, and from 1916 leader of the House of Commons.

In March, 1921, he suffered from ill health and retired, but returned in the spring of 1922 and in the General Election of that year was elected by the Unionist Party as Prime Minister.

Ill-health, however, continued to dog him at the height of his career and in May, 1923, he resigned to seek health on the Riviera, but died in London the following October.

Two of his sons died in the war while one, Richard, followed him into politics as MP for South-West Hull.

Bonar Law also was Prime Minister at the time of formation of the now right wing 1922 Committee, a fact given an airing recently by Alistair Cooke in a letter to the Daily Telegraph. The November, 1922, General Election produced a large number of new Conservative MPs - 111 out of 345 - and many of them, came to the conclusion that they needed a forum to help them overcome the handicap of parliamentary experience, which Bonar Law himself had overcome through his involvement with the Glasgow Parliamentary Debating Association. This was duly formed in April the following year.

One wonders if, in the five months between Bonar Law's resignation and his death when he must have reflected on his life, there was a small place in his memory for Helensburgh Golf Club. Surely there was, and his own brief involvement is a fascinating addition to our own history.

DOUGLAS DALGLEISH
"A man of conviction"

The rise of Douglas Dalgleish to vice-president of the Scottish Golf Union and scheduled to be president in 1994, when he will be the first Helensburgh member to be so honoured, can be traced back to his involvement with the Helensburgh Boys Open.

Son Colin was a county B player on the verge of a breakthrough into the A team and Douglas was acting as chauffeur on the away matches.

On one such occasion he was approached by the then president of Dumbartonshire, David Calder, and secretary Bob Jenkins and asked if they could have a quiet word with him the following week at Cathcart Castle.

It was there that Douglas was told that his work with the boys open had so impressed them that they thought he was an eminently suitable person to join the county executive committee and that if he was willing to do so could he arrive at the agm at Clydebank & District the following Wednesday half an hour early.

Douglas duly arrived at the appointed hour and was presented by Bob Jenkins with the script of what was to happen. It was only when he browsed through this document that he discovered he was actually being nominated for vice-president which meant, in the natural course of events, that he would be president two years hence.

This office coincided with his vice-captaincy at Helensburgh which further meant that he would be club captain and county president at the same time - and there was more to come. In 1980 he was invited to be the county representative on the Scottish Golf Union.

This sequence of events all led up to the unique situation when Colin won the Scottish Amateur Championship in 1981 that Douglas happened to be a) his father; b) the captain of his golf club; c) the president of his county; and d) his representative on the Scottish Golf Union.

It was as clear a case as there could be of keeping everything in the family and this compelling rise to the top continued apace, though it must be said this was entirely off the course.

Learning to play golf at the same time as his wife, May, and sons Colin and Gordon, Douglas, who was yet to discover his talents lay in administration and after dinner speaking, was later to tell the story against himself that even by combining the handicaps of his wife and two sons, then doubling the total, he would still be receiving strokes.

May and Douglas Dalgleish: Their decision to become involved in golf as a family in 1969 was to have a tremendous impact both on the club and beyond.

For a period of 10 years after Colin's success, Douglas made himself known in SGU circles with a forceful style. If things happened in the SGU that he did not think were right he said so in no uncertain terms which raised many an eyebrow because few officials had ever acted in this manner.

What particularly irked him, and still does, was the way in which decisions were sometimes taken without any reference whatsoever to the executive committee, and by speaking out whenever this happened he believed he was destined never to become president having rubbed up so many people the wrong way.

He was to be proved wrong in that respect, and Douglas Rae, of Greenock, invited our man in 1991 to follow him on the road to the president's chair.

It is clear that the SGU had seen beyond the sometimes brash exterior and to a man whose heart and soul is in the game.

In 1994 it will be the role of others to make a critical appraisal of the president-to-be's declared objective of making the Scottish Golf Union more meaningful to the average club golfer.

Douglas was sponsorship and public relations convener for many years, and was involved in the introduction of J & B as backers of the Scottish Amateur Championship and Scottish Golfer of the Year order of merit and the establishment of the Scottish Golfer, the monthly SGU publication.

A lawyer by profession, making him a man of conviction in more ways than one, Douglas also has brought his company, Brunton Miller, to the fore in the club by sponsoring and organising the imaginative and popular winter league competition, but his contribution to the club has gone far beyond that.

His powers of persuasion were never more evident than the special meeting held in the Victoria Halls in 1991 at which he persuaded members that the way forward was to sell the lower portion of the course for housing to raise funds for a new clubhouse and to develop the presently unused land to a total of 27 holes.

This was not the first time he had taken steps to secure the future of the club as in 1978 he played a key role in the purchase of the course from Luss Estates, an episode detailed in Chapter 2.

At the 99th AGM in Jan 1993, Douglas was made an Honorary Member of Helensburgh Golf Club, and for the first time ever, he did not speak out!

CHAPTER 8

Trophies and winners

BEN MURRAY: BIGGEST HIT OF THE MAJOR WINNERS

LENGTH of history and consistency of purpose as well as prestige are the factors determining the status of competitions as the professional "majors" as in The Open Championship, the US Open, the US Masters and the US PGA Championship. Which, then, are the Helensburgh Golf Club majors?

In the men's section the Hood Trophy for the club championship must be declared the No.1 even though its inception at 1924 makes it far from the oldest. That distinction goes to the Breingan Medal which is unique in the trophy cabinet as the only item which is as old as the club itself. It was played for in the first competitive year of the club, 1894, and with the exception of the Second World War its record is complete. The Breingan Medal can therefore be declared a major and we will add the Anderson Cup (1922), Ormond Medal (1939), all medal competitions with a pedigree, and the Colgrain Cup (1901), which has been handicap singles matchplay for its duration. The date of the Ormond Medal is slightly misleading as it had two direct predecessors which were won outright, and the competition can be considered as dating back to 1912. No others fit the bill, so we will stop the list at five and proceed with the serious business of determining who in the club has won the most majors.

That honour goes to **Ben Murray** on a total of 13 (Hood, 1926, 1930, 1931, 1935; Breingan 1927, 1928, 1934, 1936, 1939; Anderson 1933; Colgrain 1926, 1928, 1935). That record, however, is in danger of being beaten as there are three players on a total of 11, two of them still active.

Ben Murray: His total of 13 "majors" was completed in 1939.

69 HELENSBURGH GOLF CLUB CENTENARY

On 11 are **Mac Stewart** (Hood 1957, 1958, 1959; Breingan 1968; Anderson 1954, 1957, 1971; Ormond 1956, 1958; Colgrain 1957, 1971), a haul which may be considered complete as he is in his sixties and no longer plays. On the same total, however, are **John Munro** (Hood 1953, 1960, 1961, 1964, 1967; Breingan 1972; Anderson 1953, 1961; Ormond 1966; Colgrain 1961, 1981) and **Evan McGregor** (Hood 1970, 1983, 1984; Breingan 1967, 1969, 1990; Anderson 1982; Ormond 1974; Colgrain 1959, 1967, 1978). On eight majors is **Iain McCulloch** (Hood 1956, 1965, 1968; Ormond 1954, 1968, 1970; Colgrain 1965, 1974). This trio, although past their prime, remain formidable competitors and it might be premature to declare their accounts closed.

If there are any doubts in this respect, it is not the case with **Colin Dalgleish** on nine, eight of which are the Hood Trophy plus the 1975 Colgrain Cup and **Fraser McCathie** on eight, of which six are the Hood Trophy, the other two being the Anderson Cup in 1980 and Ormond Medal in 1976. It will be a surprise if these totals do not rise.

winning net scores lower than the course record. Stewart, Munro and McGregor are the only players to have won all five at one time or another. It might be slightly unfair to exclude Murray because the Ormond Medal was introduced only in 1939, and therefore he had little opportunity to win it. As far as we can gather from the records, though, he failed to win either of its predecessors the Invergare and McDonald medals.

Murray is still remembered by some of the older members as having a reputation for hitting phenomenal shots, and at one time there was a suggestion that a memorial stone be located in the left rough of the 14th between the gully and the first bunker. After a poor drive into a bad lie, Murray is said to have reached the green some 300 yards away with his second shot, an amazing strike especially considering the equipment of the time.

The four times champion was born in Dornoch in 1891 and came to Helensburgh about 1927 to work with O B Ross, shoemakers, and joined the club straightaway. He is said to have been a quiet man but beneath that

Four of Helensburgh's finest: Mac Stewart (above left), Iain McCulloch (centre), Evan McGregor (top right), and John Munro (bottom right). All have been club champions and together they have collected no fewer than 41 club "majors".

No player has won the Grand Slam, and it is unlikely that this feat will ever be achieved because to win the Hood Trophy a player will almost certainly require a low handicap which will reduce their chances of winning the others as higher handicappers are ever likely to post

exterior was a fearsome competitor who latterly at any rate appears to have suffered problems with his putting and was frequently to be seen bent almost double and gripping the shaft no more than 12 inches from the ground.

He might have won even more than he did but for a decision, for whatever reason, of opting out of competitions in the late forties and choosing instead to play only bounce golf. Murray was a highly accomplished player at Dornoch before he came to Helensburgh.

Dornoch did not have a club championship until 1959 but on two occasion at least he reached the final of the club's six day open scratch tournament for the Carnegie Shield, the first the year before he came south and once later. He is still remembered in Dornoch for coming home every year to compete.

Munro is rated by his contemporaries as a redoubtable competitor and the finest iron player in the club until the arrival of McCathie. He was born in Cumnock, Ayrshire, and came to the town as a policeman.

He was also a fine athlete, having won the West of Scotland Junior 100 yards title, and his best time for the 100 yards was an impressive 10 seconds flat. He was also a champion bowler, twice winning the British Police Championship and reaching the final of the Scottish singles at Queen's Park in the 1950s. Beyond the golf club itself he was a county player, a winner of the Scottish Police Championship and four times runner-up in the British Police Championship.

McCulloch joined the club in 1948 as a 14 year old at a time when there were only two medal rounds a year for juniors, the Paul Medal and the Captain's Prize, and as a further measure of the consideration given to juniors in those days he was denied entry into the club championship of 1952 because he was 14 days below the minimum age limit of 18. Largely self-taught, although he did have a lesson once from S B Wallace, the professional at Cardross, he made up for this under-age exclusion by winning the championship firstly in 1956, the first 36 hole final, in which he defeated Jimmy Stewart after having been one down at the halfway stage. It was ample revenge for the reversal the previous year at the hands of Stewart in what was to be the last 18-hole final.

He was briefly a county player, his team mates including twice Scottish Amateur champion Dr. Frank Deighton, and was and still is known as a short game artist capable of getting up and down from the most unlikely of positions. Golf beyond club level came to a halt, however, in 1958 when he started up his business as a painter and decorator. He twice created course records of 69 and then 67 at a time when the par of the course was 71.

Stewart was regarded as a precise, neat and accurate player with a two-thirds swing featuring a characteristic pause at the top and a highly competitive nature but modest with it.

There were no triumphal utterings after his run of three championships from 1957, and when he was eliminated by McCulloch in the semi-finals in 1960 his attitude was typical. "I knew I was lucky these past three years," he told McCulloch.

Stewart's grandfather owned the Stewarts of Jedburgh knitwear firm and Mac himself had entrepreneurial flair, having businesses in Campbeltown and Glasgow - where did he find time for golf? - before reverting to the traditional family business and opening his knitwear shop in Helensburgh.

McGregor's strength, like McCulloch, was in his short game and he had a long wait before his name appeared on the champion's board having been beaten finalist on five occasions before his first success in 1970. McGregor, who ran a bakery in between playing golf was victorious twice more in 1983 and 1984 which were all the more notable for breaking the stranglehold on the championship by Dalgleish and McCathie.

HOOD TROPHY (CLUB CHAMPIONSHIP)
The men's Club Championship competition was inaugurated in 1924, and two years later the officers of H M S Hood presented a trophy in appreciation of the welcome they experienced at the club. The warship at this time was frequently anchored on the Clyde near the town and during these periods Helensburgh Golf Club extended the courtesy of the course to its officers, as the club appears to have done as a matter of course for all visiting ships.

The story of H M S Hood is even more gripping than the history of our club, and we are grateful to Ian Bruce, defence correspondent of The Herald, for the following account:

"H M S Hood, known as "The Mighty Hood" was the embodiment of British sea power between the wars, but she was, in reality, an old lady by the outbreak of the Second World War. The 42,000-ton battlecruiser was the biggest warship ever built. Laid down in 1916 at John Brown's yard on the Clyde, she was launched in 1918 just three months before the Armistice ended the First World War.

She was armed with eight 15-inch main guns, each of which threw shells weighing a ton apiece. She could slice through the water at 32 knots, which also made her the fastest warship of her class, but it took a ton of oil to drive her only half a mile at full speed. Her Achilles heel was the armour plating on her upper decks. While the sides of the vessel were up to 13 inches thick to withstand the heaviest of enemy shellfire, the deck protection was as little as 3.5 inches in places.

She was named after a family who had given Britain four famous admirals. Lord Hood helped Rodney defeat the French at the West Indies in the late 1700s. His brother, Lord Bridgport, was the Admiral Howe at the Glorious First of June, another French defeat during the Napoleonic wars. Sam Hood helped Nelson win the battle of the Nile, and Horace Hood was killed at Jutland during the First World War - prophetically when his flagship, the Invincible, was hit by German shellfire and blew up. H M S Hood was launched by his widow in August, 1918.

Between the wars, when a quarter of the globe was still coloured red for the British Empire, the Hood showed the flag throughout the world. Her 1923-24 tour (sorry, nae T-shirts to commemorate the gig) together with H M S Repulse and five cruisers, was described as the most successful cruise by a squadron of warships in the history of sea power. She visited ports from Zanzibar to Newfoundland and was seen by millions during the 11-month voyage.

Her doom came on May 24, 1941, at 6 am, when she and H M S Prince of Wales found the Bismarck and her escort the Prinz Eugen in the Denmark Strait between Greenland and Iceland. Almost all of the Royal Navy's might was concentrated on finding and destroying the Bismarck, then the most formidable fighting ship afloat, as she broke out into the Atlantic to savage the vital convoys coming across from Canada and the USA.

On that fatal morning, the British opened fire first, targeting both German ships at a range of about 13 miles through a grey squall and heavy seas. Bismarck and Prinz Eugen immediately returned the salvo, concentrating on the Hood instead of splitting their fire. Hood took several hits, one of which started a fire on her boat deck. German rangefinding equipment was superior, and their shells were striking the target more often than the British.

Then, less than 20 minutes after the battle started, a salvo of 15-inch shells from the Bismarck straddled the Hood, throwing up great plumes of water. But one shell plunged down through the weakly-armoured upper deck and exploded in a magazine. The resultant blast triggered off a second, devastating blast in the aft 15-inch magazine. Onlookers on the German warships and on the Prince of Wales watched as the Hood literally disintegrated, split in two, and plunged beneath the waves. Only three survivors from a crew of 95 officers and 1324 other ranks were recovered from the water. As the fore section of the ship slid under, her two forward turrets sent out a last defiant salvo, probably the result of seawater triggering the guns' electrical firing circuits.

The Prince of Wales moved off smartly and rapidly behind a smokescreen and the battle was temporarily over. It later turned out that shells from the British ships had damaged one of the Bismarck's fuel tanks, allowing it to become contaminated by seawater. The resultant cut in her speed allowed other British warships to catch and sink her a few days later."

Battle, meanwhile, continued apace for the Hood Trophy and though never in quite such a violent manner it was still with all the accuracy of the Bismarck as the club's top players peppered the greens in pursuit of the top prize.

The competition has always been a scratch event with qualifying medal rounds followed by matchplay although the rules have changed from time to time, variously having 8, 12 and 16 qualifiers. Occasionally, as now, the holder has been an automatic qualifier. In the early days the final was over 18 holes but since the 1950s it has been over 36 holes except in special circumstances. For many years the qualifying route was via the best two out of three rounds in nominated Breingan and Anderson medals but because of various difficulties the competition was recently restructured as 36 holes of strokeplay, for which there is a prize of a salver, followed by matchplay. Weather permitting, the competition takes place during an eight-day period, Sunday to Sunday.

The Champions' Board reveals some interesting highlights such as R R Herbertson and I L B McCulloch being the only two captains to win. Colin Dalgleish, with eight wins, has moved ahead of Fraser McCathie, who has six, and we are sure these are not the final figures for the pair. Dalgleish, at the age of 32, is already the multiple winner with the longest gap between his first and most recent triumphs, currently 15 years (1977-1992). This is one more than both John Munro (1953-1967) and Evan McGregor (1970-1984).

Many of the champions have been written about above. Of the remainder, the first winner was the minister at St Columba's, the Reverend J Walker. His golfing heyday is beyond living memory which for him is a pity because he will forever be remembered as the man who, of a Monday on his day off, had a large whisky served to him in a glass of milk lest his parishioners think the worse of him.

The next champion, R R Herbertson, was by all accounts a pillar of Helensburgh society, a former provost and a man who ruled the clubhouse with an iron fist. Juniors walked in fear and trepidation of this strict disciplinarian who was captain within a year of being club champion and then went on to become president, after many active years as greens convener.

One of the great club characters, Johnny Rafferty, came to the fore in 1929. He was a ticket collector at the station and his shiftwork enabled him to play much golf. He was ever willing to impart advice to fellow members on how to improve their swings and was an

The Reverend J Walker: Helensburgh's first club champion.

avid practiser, often when he should not have been, on one occasion having to be reprimanded for hitting some 20 balls on to the eighteenth green.

In 1932 it was the turn of Stewart McNeil, an uncle of Evan McGregor. He came from Port Glasgow and began the bakery business, G & S McNeil, which McGregor later took over. McNeil was a good all round player with an unerring putting touch.

The success of Lennox Paterson came at an early age and he then left the town later to become deputy head of Glasgow Art School. He returned to Helensburgh but did not rejoin the golf club.

Stanley McElroy, three times a winner, was the brother of Phil McElroy, the professional at Buchanan Castle who had among his assistants one Eric Brown. Stanley might have won more but for the outbreak of war during which he spent more than three years in captivity in a Japanese prison of war camp. He survived to tell the tale and was able to resume his golf, later joining the Glasgow club.

Campbell Steven, the 1938 champion, was a writer and broadcaster while twice winner Bill Jardine was a banker who later went east and played out of Edzell. Billy Forsyth, the 1950 and 1954 champion, was a painter who was as skilled with a mashie as he was with a paintbrush and was noted on the course for a round, full and rhythmic swing.

Alistair McKillop was introduced to golf by Bob Ralph. Previously he had played football as a forward under manager Bill Struth at Rangers and then at Morton. A plumber by trade, he took to golf with great enthusiasm and practised untiringly to develop a short, punchy swing. By nature he was extremely competitive which made him better at matchplay in which he knew what he had to do and he was champion twice before emigrating to Australia.

Jimmy Stewart, the 1955 champion, was a streak player able to scale the heights as well as plumb the depths. He once broke Tom Haliburton's record of 27 at Shandon by one shot, a score of one under threes for the nine holes, and he came closer than the records might suggest to winning the Scottish Amateur Championship of 1957 at Balgownie where he reached the last 16 only to lose to eventual winner John Montgomerie. Stewart's confidence had been increasing round by round and his exit was in some ways unfortunate as at one hole on the inward half he was lying handily on the green with Montgomerie facing an awkward pitch over a bunker which he holed only for Stewart to miss the putt. That could be regarded as a two-hole swing accounting for the 2 and 1 reversal.

William Thornton, a dedicated golfer and a perfectionist, was, notwithstanding Morty Dykes, the first Helensburgh member to be selected for a national squad and was capped both at boy and youth level. A graduate in law and accountancy he was also to become a highly successful businessman in the whisky trade. Three times the club champion, he was reminded abruptly after his last triumph just how precarious is the mantle of champion. "It's tough at the top," he is recalled to have said after having been defeated by Evan McGregor, who instantly reminded him: "You're no longer at the top." This remark had nothing to do with Thornton's later decision to join Cardross, which he considered to be a better course, and where he later became captain.

Ian Still, the winner in 1963, was a prodigious striker of the ball able to reach both the fifth and 12th greens with a drive, the latter off what is now the forward tee. He had a splendid, long swing, though occasionally with a tendency to hook. He was an accountant, who later emigrated to Canada, and one anecdote we have about him concerns an object lesson he received in profit and loss from Evan McGregor, who, as we have already recorded, once put William Thornton in his place.

Still had arrived for a game without a ball in his bag and, having searched in the woods to the left of the first without success, asked McGregor for a loan. "I'll sell you one," said his opponent, never one to miss an opportunity, and a Warwick was duly supplied for ninepence. Still's hook was obviously behaving itself and the ball lasted the round whereupon he piped up: "I'm a wee bit short, would you like to buy the ball back?"

McGregor examined the ball like an archaeologist looking at a relic from an Egyptian tomb, and pointing out that it was not quite in the same condition as before, said: "I'll give you threepence for it."

In 1966, chemist John Fairlie laid the ghost of a previous final defeat at the hands of John Munro who had unnerved him by hooking out of bounds at the third only for the ball to strike a tree and come back into play, to earn his place on the Champion's Board before moving down south to Welwyn Garden City, home of Nick Faldo.

Peter Reece, another who transferred allegiance to Cardross (there's no accounting for taste), won the first of his three crowns in 1969, defeating Martin Gray who, the previous day, had lost in the final of the British Boys' Championship. Reece, a member of the building trade, was, and still is, an exceptionally fine player and held the course record of 64 in 1969 prior to the lengthening of the 10th and 12th holes. His compact swing remains in evidence as some find to their cost in the McIntyre League.

David Weir was one of a group of enthusiastic and skillful players including John Lennox, Paul Stevens, Graham Heron, and Ally Buchan who either moved away or gave up the game, in Weir's case to pursue a career in the insurance business. Weir had a golden period in the mid-1970s during which he won the championship twice and also the Dumbartonshire Strokeplay Championship at Helensburgh with a two round score of 135 (66,69). The late Andrew Turnbull from Garelochhead once described Weir's swing as "good for hammering in fence stabs," but his method was certainly successful.

The Hood Trophy.

1924 Rev J W Walker	1962 W Thornton
1925 R R Herbertson	1963 I McK Still
1926 Ben Murray	1964 John Munro
1927 I H McKenzie	1965 I L B McCulloch
1928 L G Whyte	1966 J Fairlie
1929 J Rafferty	1967 John Munro
1930 Ben Murray	1968 I L B McCulloch
1931 Ben Murray	1969 P B Reece
1932 W S McNeil	1970 E H McGregor
1933 Lennox Paterson	1971 P B Reece
1934 D B McDonald	1972 W Thornton
1935 Ben Murray	1973 W Thornton
1936 F S McElroy	1974 D W Weir
1937 F S McElroy	1975 P B Reece
1938 C M Steven	1976 D W Weir
1939 F S McElroy	1977 C R Dalgleish
1947 W Jardine	1978 C R Dalgleish
1948 J M Dykes	1979 R F B McCathie
1949 W Jardine	1980 C R Dalgleish
1950 W Forsyth	1981 C R Dalgleish
1951 A McKillop	1982 C R Dalgleish
1952 A McKillop	1983 E H McGregor
1953 John Munro	1984 E H McGregor
1954 W Forsyth	1985 R F B McCathie
1955 J Stewart	1986 R F B McCathie
1956 I L B McCulloch	1987 R F B McCathie
1957 A A M Stewart	1988 C R Dalgleish
1958 A A M Stewart	1989 R F B McCathie
1959 A A M Stewart	1990 R F B McCathie
1960 John Munro	1991 C R Dalgleish
1961 John Munro	1992 C R Dalgleish

BREINGAN MEDAL

This is undoubtedly the oldest trophy in the club's possession and was presented in 1894 by the first captain of Helensburgh Golf Club, Alexander Breingan.

From the sparse records now available to us, it seems that until 1921 this medal competition was restricted to low handicap players. There is a clue in that the agm of winter 1921-22 ruled that in future the competition would in future be open to all ordinary members and therefore we can assume that previously the field was restricted.

The Breingan Medal is normally played on the first Saturday of each month with a final among the monthly qualifiers - one each month from each class - held in September. Nowadays there are only nine such monthly medals from March through November with September, October and November qualifiers competing in the final of the following season.

There is a recent instance of three generations of the same family having win the medal. Sinclair Mackay, donor of the junior Mackay Cup, won in 1935, followed by his son Dan in 1950. In 1987 it was the turn of Alistair McKenzie, who is married to Dan's niece, Wilma.

The Breingan Medal.

1894 Robert Whyte	1947 G Hamilton
1895 John Brash	1948 J G Holland
1896 John Brash	1949 J Cumming
1897 John G Ure	1950 D Mackay
1898 John G Ure	1951 W Forsyth
1899 John G Ure	1952 F Kerr
1900 G H McParlane	1953 Ian Macdonald
1901 W H Kidston	1954 M Rafferty
1902 John Dingwall	1955 R Osborne
1904 R T Templeton	1956 J O Smith
1905 Ian Ure	1957 I McK Still
1906 Dugald Bannatyne	1958 J H M Green
1907 Eric W Mackay	1959 D L Dods
1908 Eric W Mackay	1960 K Blackwell
1909 Hew T Young	1961 Dr A G Miller
1910 Robert Stanton	1962 R McK Douglas
1911 John G Ure	1963 G Park
1912 George Hamilton	1964 R McK Douglas
1913 R O Elder	1965 J A Spy
1914 J R Martin Jr	1966 A C Lochhead
1915 J S McDonald	1967 E H McGregor
1916 R O Elderton	1968 A A M Stewart
1917 Andrew Kyle	1969 E H McGregor
1918 T N Perkins	1970 R J Dunn
1919 A G Macaslan	1971 R E Petrie
1920 J Morrison	1972 John Munro
1921 J A D McElroy	1973 D M Griffiths
1922 A H Paterson	1974 D W Weir
1923 John Porter	1975 W J McPherson
1924 A Thomson	1976 T Griffiths
1925 G Fairbairn	1977 P G Stevens
1926 David L Dods	1978 H S Orr
1927 Ben Murray	1979 C Cameron
1928 Ben Murray	1980 D Westwater
1929 Wm Crossan	1981 A Dunlop
1930 F S McElroy	1982 D Carswell
1931 D B Macdonald	1983 J Fraser
1932 David L Dods	1984 K G Hale
1933 David L Dods	1985 J Shaw
1934 Ben Murray	1986 F Goodfellow
1935 S Mackay	1987 A C McKenzie
1936 Ben Murray	1988 J Stephenson
1937 J B Michie Jr	1989 A Ross
1938 Arthur McCulloch	1990 E H McGregor
1939 Ben Murray	1991 T M Griffiths
1946 Robert Biggar	1992 Peter Mundie

ANDERSON CUP

This trophy was presented in the winter of 1921-22 by R L Anderson. The records suggest that for some years this was another monthly medal competition, again on the first Saturday of each month but restricted to second-class players. In 1930 the competition had been changed to play against bogey (or par nowadays) and was held on the third Saturday of each month. It seems that the Anderson Cup was then open to all ordinary members and remained a bogey competition at least until 1938. Today the cup is played for under the same rules as the Breingan Medal with monthly qualifiers and the final in September.

1922 Rev Stephen Band	1961 John Munro
1923 Colin R Hamilton	1962 J B Shearer
1924 John Rowan	1963 J Fairlie
1925 John Rowan	1964 R Baynham
1926 John Rafferty	1965 J C Fairlie
1927 Thomas Cooke	1966 J S Dow
1928 R R Herbertson	1967 J M MacLachlan
1929 F S McElroy	1968 D W Elliot
1930 Walter M Bryden	1969 J S G Lennox
1931 George N Begley	1970 W Parkhouse
1932 David L Dods	1971 A A M Stewart
1933 Ben Murray	1972 G Turnbull
1934 F S McElroy	1973 D W Weir
1935 F S McElroy	1974 A Kelly
1936 F S McElroy	1975 F J Prime
1937 J G Troup	1976 G D Dalgleish
1938 D Beavis	1977 M Kelly
1939 E Murray	1978 E McLean
1947 W Jardine	1979 T L Hamilton
1948 R Ralph	1980 R F B McCathie
1949 J Crossan	1981 G Perella
1950 J C Fraser	1982 E H McGregor
1951 R Ralph	1983 W Farrell
1952 D White	1984 J S Christie
1953 John Munro	1985 R Burns
1954 A A M Stewart	1986 F Goodfellow
1955 J D Beveridge	1987 C Cameron
1956 R Robertson	1988 D Reid
1957 A A M Stewart	1989 W Petrie
1958 R Livingston	1990 C F Barbour
1959 R A Peel	1991 R Burns
1960 T Bonning	1992 G Gill

INVERGARE CHALLENGE, McDONALD AND ORMOND MEDALS

In 1912, James Macdonald of Invergare, Row (Rhu), presented the Invergare Challenge Medal for competition by ordinary members on the last Wednesday of each month. In 1922-23 James S McDonald of Methilfield won the Invergare medal for the third time which meant outright in those days. He immediately presented the McDonald Medal in its place. The McDonald Medal was last played for in May, 1938, when it appears to have been won outright by T S McArthur, who defeated W S McNeil in a play-off. McArthur, notably, was also the first winner of the Ormond Medal.

The Ormond Medal is attributed to H H Ormond, for many years an active member and secretary, and is the modern Wednesday Medal. There are six monthly qualifying rounds, April through to September, with the final play-off normally in June. There is, of course, the curiosity that four of the six qualifying rounds belong to the preceding season and as a further quirk the dates of the winners are engraved as the year before the actual final. It is perhaps worth commenting that if the tradition of the previous two trophies had continued, the Ormond Medal would have been won outright by Iain McCulloch in 1970, or should it be 1971?

(Invergare)

1913 J A D McElroy	1919 N Campbell
1914 J S McDonald	1920 A C Macaslan
1915 A McDougall	1921 A C Macaslan
1916 J S McDonald	1922 A H Paterson
1917 W C McLean	1923 J S McDonald
1918 T T N Perkins	

(McDonald)

1924 J Campbell	1932 W Donaldson
1925 Rev J W Walker	1933 L Paterson
1926 S K Mackay	1934 W D B Tennant
1927 W S Lowe	1935 T G McArthur
1928 W Watson	1936 T G McArthur
1929 D Shields	1937 W S McNeil
1930 W Crossan	1938 T G McArthur
1931 A G Miller	

(Ormond)

1939 T G McArthur	1968 I L B McCulloch
1940 I W Purvis	1969 D Millar
1946 Charles Friel	1970 I L B McCulloch
1947 R Ralph	1971 D H Davidson
1948 J Fraser	1972 J V L Miller
1949 W Rae	1973 G Mickel
1950 J Cummings	1974 E H McGregor
1951 R G Hattle	1975 D Donaldson
1952 D L Ralph	1976 R F M McCathie
1953 F Shields	1977 P K Mill
1954 I L B McCulloch	1978 B R Mill
1955 F Shields	1979 G Mickel
1956 A A M Stewart	1980 C Cameron
1957 A Osborne	1981 C Cameron
1958 A A M Stewart	1982 M D Carlisle
1959 H Welsh	1983 D M Park
1960 J Munro	1984 G Gill
1961 R G Hattle	1985 J Cavana
1962 R McK Douglas	1986 N Prime
1963 E H McGregor	1987 M Anderson
1964 R Gordon	1988 K L Curtis
1965 J Fullerton	1989 D H Gethin
1966 J Munro	1990 A Catterson
1967 J Lillburn	1991 M Currie

MILLIGAN CUP

Early records indicate that special prizes were awarded for the best aggregates based on the four best net scores in medal rounds. In recent years an aggregate prize has been awarded for the best aggregate net score in the Breingan, Anderson and Ormond medals. The task of finding the winner is invariably a challenge to the match and handicap secretary.

In 1983 the widow of James Milligan presented a cup which was assigned to the aggregate competition.

1983 G Miller	1988 G W Beattie
1984 G Henderson	1989 W Beck
1985 R Gudge	1990 R Rogers
1986 G Platt	1991 G Gill
1987 C Cameron	1992 F Goodfellow

COLGRAIN CHALLENGE CUP

This is another early trophy presented by Wm Middleton Campbell of Colgrain and was first played for in 1901. The competition is singles matchplay and in the early years was confined to the months of May and June. Nowadays, with a greater number of entrants, the competition generally runs from April through to September.

There is an early reference to another matchplay tournament confined to players with handicaps of 10 or more and it may be that the Colgrain Challenge Cup once had a low handicap restriction though we do not know this for sure.

It is interesting to note that Ian Macdonald won this trophy in 1953 and again in 1991 - a span of 39 years. Equally notable is the fact that Bob Ralph was the winner in 1987 at the age of 76.

1901 John G Ure	1952 K W Angus
1902 Douglas McIntyre	1953 Ian Macdonald
1903 E M Raeburn	1954 M Rafferty
1904 R L D Kidston	1955 A M McKillop

1905 T M Lunan
1906 William Bryden
1907 H B Kidston
1908 Robert Stanton
1909 Ian Ure
1910 James MacDougall
1911 A G Cruickshank
1912 E W Mackay
1913 J A D McElroy
1914 Robert Stanton
1919 J S McDonald
1920 J A D McElroy
1921 Alex MacDougall
1922 George A Paterson
1923 Robert Stanton
1924 Allan M Duncan
1925 A Thomson
1926 Ben Murray
1927 L G Whyte
1928 Ben Murray
1929 A Thomson
1930 D J de M Beaumont
1931 W S McNeil
1932 Lennox Paterson
1933 Lennox Paterson
1934 C R Steven
1935 Ben Murray
1936 M B Wedgewood
1937 Robert Biggar
1938 D Beavis
1939 W J Beaumont
1946 Charles Friel
1947 W Jardine
1948 J B Michie
1949 W S McNeil
1950 K W Angus
1951 W McKenzie

1956 J Cummings
1957 A A M Stewart
1958 M M Watson
1959 E H McGregor
1960 R Dewar
1961 J Munro
1962 J McAuley
1963 J Fairlie
1964 George Park
1965 I L B McCulloch
1966 J B Stewart
1967 E H McGregor
1968 W Thornton
1969 W Fyfe
1970 N S Addison
1971 A A M Stewart
1972 A J Lawson
1973 P G Stevens
1974 I L B McCulloch
1975 C R Dalgleish
1976 D Griffiths
1977 A J Green
1978 E H McGregor
1979 B D Robertson
1980 J M Graham
1981 J Munro
1982 W Cairns
1983 G Parker
1984 J E Christie
1985 J Fraser
1986 D Reid
1987 R Ralph
1988 N McFarlane
1989 J Grierson
1990 M J Tait
1991 I Macdonald
1992 L Munro

1969 J Baillie
1970 A Turnbull
1971 J Baillie
1972 S Robertson
1973 G Turnbull
1974 I B Baird
1975 I B Baird
1976 J Binner
1977 J MacLachlan
1978 J MacLachlan
1979 T Adair

1982 R Ralph
1983 R D Phoenix
1984 R Ralph
1985 R Ralph
1986 J Cameron
1987 J Munro
1988 J Munro
1989 I L B McCulloch
1990 T J Strange
1991 C J S Smith
1992 W Fyfe

KERR THOMSON TROPHY

This is the annual gents fourball matchplay competition which began in 1970 and is played on a knockout basis throughout the summer months. Blair Thomson presented the trophy in memory of his son, Kerr, who died in a road accident.

1970	E H McGregor and J B Stewart
1971	P G Stevens and N S Addison
1972	A S Buchan and J S G Lennox
1973	J D Steele and J S Craig
1974	E H McGregor and J B Stewart
1975	R B Gall and A McAdam
1976	I L B McCulloch and J Munro
1977	D W Weir and D Griffiths
1978	E H McGregor and J B Stewart
1979	E H McGregor and J B Stewart
1980	C Cameron and W Petrie
1981	I L B McCulloch and J Munro
1982	E H McGregor and A Scott
1983	E H McGregor and A Scott
1984	E H McGregor and A Scott
1985	G Beattie and J Stark
1986	W Trail and A McKenzie
1987	R Prow and J Ramsay
1988	A S Harper and J Ford
1989	R F B McCathie and A Dunlop
1990	J Fugler and I McKenna
1991	S M Gethin and S Farrow
1992	A S Harper and J Ford

SENIORS QUAICH

Known nowadays as the McIlraith Trophy, it was presented by former captain John McIlraith in 1967 for senior competition. Eligibility requires the gentlemen to be aged 55 or over on the first day of the financial year, that is November 1. For some years there were qualifying rounds based on Breingan or Anderson medals leading to a final in September.

Today the competition comprises one round only combined with a selected Breingan or Anderson medal.

1967 W Walker
1968 R A Peel

1980 R D Phoenix
1981 J Munro

BLAIR LOMOND CUP

The gents foursomes matchplay competition began in 1962 with the trophy presented by the former Luss Estates factor, Charles F Swain. The knockout format operates on the same basis as the Kerr Thomson Trophy.

1962	W S McNeil and J Munro
1963	I Macdonald and G Park

1964	I Macdonald and G Park
1965	I L B McCulloch and J Spy
1966	J Fullerton and E Davis
1967	R Simpson and D S Rodger
1968	W S McNeil and J Munro
1969	D E Carswell and G Fraser Jr
1970	K W Angus and A A M Stewart
1971	P G Stevens and J S G Lennox
1972	J A McAuley and D M Robertson
1973	I L B McCulloch and J Munro
1974	C R Dalgleish and J McAuley
1975	R B Gall and A Adam
1976	C R Dalgleish and C Sinclair
1977	C R Dalgleish and C Sinclair
1978	E J Boyle and A Scott
1979	C C Sinclair and T S Anderson
1980	I L B McCulloch and J Munro
1981	J Graham and R Howarth
1982	I L B McCulloch and J Munro
1983	G H Reid and G Miller
1984	K Reid and G Orr
1985	K Reid and G Orr
1986	G Belch and D Cochrane
1987	D Yorke and A Dunlop
1988	A B Miller and G Miller
1989	J Belch and G Belch
1990	J A P Milne and A Scott
1991	D S Craig and D G Craig
1992	G Ross and J Purdon

R A PEEL TROPHY

The trophy was presented by R A Peel for competition among second-class handicap gents. First played for in 1971, the competition rules and handicap range have been modified to suit changing circumstances. At the present time there is one round of medal play to establish 16 qualifiers who then play matchplay knockout. The competition is a scratch event with gross medal scores and level matches.

1972 P I Brown	1983 A Peebles
1973 A D G McLean	1984 R A Laurenson
1974 E J Boyle	1985 S Hannah
1975 A S Harper	1986 F Goodfellow
1976 D M Robertson	1987 D Shearer
1977 D M Robertson	1988 J Fraser
1978 P Brown	1989 A Parker
1979 T L Hamilton	1990 R Stocker
1980 J Horn	1991 C Donald
1981 R Howarth	1992 R Stocker
1982 R D Graham	

1963 TROPHY

This cup was provided by a number of low handicap players including Ian Still and Evan McGregor originally for a 72-hole strokeplay event which lasted until 1970. In 1971 its use was transferred to the third-class championship. As with the Peel Trophy, the format is medal qualifying followed by matchplay except that there are only eight places. Gross medal scores and level matchplay applies.

1963 W Thornton	1978 D Westwater
1964 W Thornton	1979 G Gill
1965 R E Young	1980 S I Colley
1966 E H McGregor	1981 J Shilp
1967 I Macdonald	1982 D Farrow
1968 W Thornton	1983 S Munro
1969 J A McAuley	1984 A W Fraser
1970 G Park	1985 F Goodfellow
1971 W S Ross	1986 G Platt
1972 T Whitton	1987 N McFarlane
1973 W Goodall	1988 H McPherson
1974 J Milne	1989 C E Nichol
1975 A Jeffrey	1990 J Rees
1976 T Smith	1991 P Mundie
1977 S Anderson	1992 D Tolhurst

SCOTT TROPHY

This was presented in 1973 by John Scott originally for a 36-hole handicap medal competition. The committee of the day viewed this prospect with some reluctance and scheduled the event for October. It was later reduced to 18 holes, partly because those who scored poorly in the first round tended not to continue. The committee have since provided a replacement cup as the original had suffered from wear and tear.

1973 K MacDougall	1983 R S D Howarth
1974 D W Weir	1984 W Hamilton
1975 D Griffiths	1985 F Goodfellow
1976 R F B McCathie	1986 J Stark
1977 G Beattie	1987 D Reid
1978 D McLeod	1988 T Griffiths
1979 G A Belch	1989 D Reid
1980 R Parkhouse	1990 G W Ross
1981 W Ritchie	1991 F Goodfellow
1982 J Cleland	1992 No Winner

CRAWFORD LOCHHEAD TROPHY

This was presented in 1983, in memory of Crawford Lochhead, for handicap medal play with a view to raising funds for cancer research.

1983 G H Reid
1984 G Miller
1985 R Gudge
1986 R Livingstone
1987 C Barbour
1988 D Reilly
1989 R Graham
1990 G Beattie
1991 A Rankin
1992 W Ross

SPRING CLEANING TROPHY
This trophy was presented by C K Nichol, for some time listed as an absent member in the 1920s. It has proved impossible to trace the origins with certainty, but the Captain's Board reveals one C A Nicholl as captain in 1910-12 and it is possible that a son or relative offered this trophy as a memorial. In April 1969 it is recorded in a minute that the Spring Cleaning Cup had been found in the house of Mr James Buchanan, Ferness, Largs. Pre-war there had been The Spring Cleaning Golf Club of Helensburgh. The Cup was retrieved and returned to us by Sir John C Denholm CBE of Glendower, Skelmorlie.

The winners' list shows that the competition originally was a singles event and was played until 1939. The trophy was resurrected in 1970 for play in the spring as an 18-hole greensome.

1928	J F Duncan
1929	R O Pott
1930	A Stewart
1931	G A Paterson
1932	L A McGregor
1933	G D Hollis
1934	J Robertson
1935	G Gray
1936	G Fairbairn
1937	R Ralston Ness
1938	G Fairbairn
1939	J Buchanan
1970	A S Buchan and J Moore
1971	I L B McCulloch and A A M Stewart
1972	J B Stewart and W Ross
1973	S McWade and J Johnston
1974	I E Stewart and T G Reid
1975	A B Frost and J D Percy
1976	W Rose and D Russell Jones
1977	D Carswell and G Fraser Jr
1978	D Lowe and P Stott
1979	J McIntyre and J V J Miller
1980	A Scott and E J Boyle
1981	M Kirk and C F Smith
1982	E McGregor and D McConnell
1983	J McIntyre and J V J Miller
1984	W Rose and D Scougall

1985	H McPherson and J Cleland
1986	R F B McCathie and J Ashworth
1987	T Reid and H Walsh
1988	N McFarlane and W McKiernan
1989	J Cavana and J Graham
1990	A Rankin and M J Tait
1991	H W Orr and G Wilson
1992	R Goodger and B Butler

McROBERT THISTLE CUP
Lady McRobert, who lost sons in World War 2, set up a trust which operates in many fields of activity. The competition is a handicap stableford, with donations to the trust which provided the trophy.

1976 D Hall
1977 M Kelly
1978 R Park
1979 M Kelly
1980 A Scott
1981 J McIntyre
1982 A Latham
1983 G Orr
1984 J E Currie
1985 J Taig
1986 R MacDougall
1987 R Buchanan
1988 J McIntyre
1989 M J Tait
1990 J McIntyre
1991 C McKerron
1992 C J Smith

ARC TROPHY
Presented by the Arthritis and Rheumatism Council (Scotland) and used for a handicap medal competition, with participant contributions to the charity.

1981 T M Griffiths
1982 R D Graham
1983 G J Parker
1984 S Coutts
1985 J Taig
1986 No Winner
1987 R Burns
1988 F Goodfellow
1989 A Reynolds
1990 S Trotman
1991 M J Tait
1992 J Chandler

JOHN McDONALD TROPHY
This was presented by wife and family, in memory of John who died on the first green. The competition is handicap fourball.

1992 L Munro and M McCann.

VILAMOURA BP TROPHY
The mixed foursomes matchplay competition was inaugurated in 1975 with the trophy presented by "Friends of Helensburgh Golf Club" namely Ian Brown and Eric Paterson. This kind gesture followed a golfing adventure in the Algarve which was enjoyed by all concerned.

1975	E H McGregor and Mrs S Reid
1976	E H McGregor and Mrs S Reid
1977	J Munro and Miss M Munro
1978	J Munro and Miss M Munro
1979	A Scott and Mrs F Scott
1980	E H McGregor and Mrs S Reid
1981	C R Dalgleish and Miss B Gilchrist
1982	A Scott and Mrs F Scott
1983	A Scott and Mrs F Scott
1984	J Belch and Mrs E Belch
1985	A Scott and Mrs F Scott
1986	J Belch and Mrs E Belch
1987	F J Prime and Mrs A Prime
1988	J Munro and Mrs M Smith
1989	J Dykes and Mrs V Dykes
1990	G Belch and Mrs M Belch
1991	G Gill and Mrs P Crawford
1992	H McKay and Mrs. A McKay

RAMSAY HOWARTH TROPHY

This trophy was presented in memory of Ramsay Howarth by his wife and family for a family foursomes competition comprising father and son, mother and daughter or other such combinations which appeared to be almost limitless in the inaugural year. In addition to immediate family there were also aunts, uncles, nieces and nephews and some of them once or twice removed but quite within the spirit of the event which has proved to be immediately popular.

1992   W Ritchie and W Ritchie

AGNES REECE: FIRST LADY

Three majors can be identified in the ladies' section. These are the Championship Cup, which although dating back only to 1958 has sufficient prestige to merit inclusion. The others are the oldest competition, the Victoria Vase (1901), the handicap championship, and the Colgrain Challenge Cup (1903), the medal handicap championship.

Top of the ladies' major winners is Agnes Reece on 13 made up of eight championships and five successes on the Colgrain, though she did miss out on the Victoria Vase. Lynn McCathie is two behind with 10 championships and a single triumph in the Victoria Vase. She is well primed to exceed the Reece total.

There are four players on a total of nine, each with a full set. They are Fiona Gilchrist, May Dalgleish and Margaret Moir, who are multiple winners of all three majors, as is Louise McAuley who has a total of seven.

On six majors and well worth a mention is A A Lamont from the early days who tallied six and never had the opportunity to win the championship.

Two great champions: Agnes Reece and Lynn McCathie on the occasion that Lynn equalled Agnes's record of eight club championships.

Tuesday is the current ladies' medal day, and setting aside such a day is a practice which has existed since before the turn of the century, although in 1896 it was a Wednesday, a day which has since been utilised by the men at least for one medal a month. The Wednesday for men has its roots in the former early closing day for local shopkeepers. Other weekdays have been used by the ladies from time to time.

Tuesday medals are also held for prizes in aid of the Royal National Lifeboat Association, Cancer Relief and the Golf Foundation as well as the ever popular Coronation Foursomes in which winners qualify for regional and national finals.

LADIES CHAMPIONSHIP CUP

This trophy was presented in 1958 by John Allison for what is thought to be the first ladies' championship, and as fate would have it, his wife won it on the first two occasions. The record of eight wins, including six in a row by Agnes Reece, stood until it was equalled in 1990 by Lynn McCathie and then beaten. Lynn has not yet managed six in a row but at the time of writing she is at five and has her chance in the centenary year.

The two best scratch scores out of three nominated medal rounds qualify players for the knockout stages contested by the seven players with the best aggregates plus the defending champion, a format which has been unchanged since the competition's inception.

1958 S E Allison	1976 M M Dalgleish
1959 S E Allison	1977 M M Dalgleish
1960 N M Miller	1978 L McCathie
1961 A Reece	1979 M Moir
1962 A Reece	1980 L McCathie
1963 A Reece	1981 E Belch
1964 A Reece	1982 L McCathie
1965 A Reece	1983 L McCathie
1966 A Reece	1984 M Moir
1967 E Graham	1985 E Belch
1968 A Reece	1986 L McCathie
1969 A Reece	1987 M M Dalgleish
1970 P L McAuley	1988 L McCathie
1971 P L McAuley	1989 L McCathie
1972 P L McAuley	1990 L McCathie
1973 F Gilchrist	1991 L McCathie
1974 F Gilchrist	1992 L McCathie
1975 F Gilchrist	

VICTORIA VASE

This is the oldest trophy which still exists, presented by John G Ure in 1901 and which, incidentally, was won by his wife Mrs I A Ure in 1904 and 1905. Such a situation was to occur again in 1958 when the Ladies' Championship Trophy was put up by John Allison and his wife, Mrs S E Allison, took custody of it for the first two years.

The earliest known competition among the ladies, incidentally, was for the brooch presented by Mrs Breingan and which was first won in September, 1895, by Miss Crum, Blairburn, who had tied with Mrs Anderson, Dalfruin, and then beaten her in a four-hole play-off taking 21 strokes. Sadly this prize is no longer in the club's possession.

The Victoria Vase is the handicap matchplay championship with the knockout rounds taking place between April and September.

1901 A A Lamont	1951 C U Laird
1902 C N Smith	1952 M L Kerr
1903 S M Raeburn	1953 G M Gibson
1904 I A Ure	1954 J R Rankin
1905 I A Ure	1955 M K Lennie
1906 A A Lamont	1956 L Smith
1907 A A Lamont	1957 S E Allison
1908 E G Paterson	1958 S MacKenzie
1909 E R Brown	1959 S MacKenzie
1910 J S Cuthbert	1960 J MacFarlane
1911 A A Lamont	1961 J R Rankin
1912 K M Adam	1962 S H Laird
1913 J L Rodger	1963 M I Burt

1914 C M Gardiner	1964 N M Miller
1915 B A Anderson	1965 E Graham
1916 A N Paterson	1966 F Gilchrist
1918 J L Rodger	1967 N M Miller
1919 P E Arkley	1968 P L McAuley
1920 E M Elderton	1969 J E Carslaw
1921 N Anderson	1970 N M Miller
1922 N Anderson	1971 J E Carslaw
1923 E G Barrie	1972 P L McAuley
1924 J L Rodger	1973 M Moir
1925 E G Barrie	1974 F Gilchrist
1926 K D Adam	1975 M Moir
1927 M D Bathgate	1976 M M Dalgleish
1928 A I Peck	1977 S A Reid
1929 K D Adam	1978 M Moir
1930 A I Peck	1979 L McCathie
1931 B Paterson	1980 F Gilchrist
1932 J D Murdoch	1981 A Van Der Lee
1933 J W Buchanan	1982 E Shepherd
1934 F H H Ronald	1983 K E Belch
1935 M MacGillivray	1984 M Smith
1936 C S Houston	1985 F Gilchrist
1937 E G S Barrie	1986 M Carlaw
1938 M A Morton	1987 A Halligan
1939 C U Laird	1988 M Dalgleish
1948 W Simons	1989 M Dalgleish
1949 S R R Biggar	1990 M Dalgleish
1950 P D Lang	1991 A K Rogers
	1992 M Moir

COLGRAIN CHALLENGE CUP

Like the men's Colgrain Challenge Cup, this trophy was presented by Wm Middleton Campbell of Colgrain. However, it was for medal play, unlike the men's one presented a year earlier in 1901 for handicap matchplay.

There are a maximum of 16 qualifiers for the final consisting of the silver and bronze winners of the second Tuesday medal of the month between March and October. There are usually less than 16 qualifiers because if a player wins on more than one occasion there are no substitutes. The final is held on the first Tuesday in May each year.

1903 A A Lamont	1954 B Hendry
1904 A A Lamont	1955 M D Forsyth
1905 K M Adam	1956 A B Porteous
1906 K M Adam	1957 M J Stewart
1907 J L Rodger	1958 C B H Speirs
1908 K M Adam	1959 A Reece
1909 M H Paterson	1960 M B Condie
1910 J L Rodger	1961 N M Miller

1911	K M Adam	1962	J R Rankin
1912	M H Porteous	1963	A Reece
1913	E B Gifford	1964	J R Adam
1914	H Bell	1965	J M Ferrie
1915	M H Paterson	1966	A Reece
1916	J L Rodger	1967	A Reece
1917	J L Rodger	1968	A Reece
1918	J L Rodger	1969	N M Miller
1919	F S MacPhee	1970	P L McAuley
1920	K M Adam	1971	M J Plenderleath
1921	E G Barrie	1972	M Moir
1924	E G Barrie	1973	P L McAuley
1926	K D Adam	1974	E Shepherd
1928	K M Adam	1975	J R Rankin
1929	J D Murdoch	1976	M C Logan
1930	M Gray	1977	M Moir
1931	G Raeburn	1978	M Moir
1932	J W Buchanan	1979	M Dalgleish
1933	J W Buchanan	1980	E Shepherd
1934	W Wedgewood	1981	M Dalgleish
1935	C S Houston	1982	B McDonald
1936	E Graham	1983	E Shepherd
1937	S Biggar	1984	F Gilchrist
1938	E C Barrie	1985	F Gilchrist
1939	N W Graham	1986	R Cox
1948	G U Laird	1987	M Carlaw
1949	A B Porteous	1988	C S Smart
1950	J MacFarlane	1989	M Belch
1951	J MacFarlane	1990	F Gilchrist
1952	M D Forsyth	1991	K Rogers
1953	G McIlraith	1992	R Cox

FOURSOMES CUP

This trophy was presented by Morag Plenderleath on the completion of her term of captaincy and is played on a matchplay basis between April and September. Morag, incidentally, has won her own trophy on four occasions and is the current holder along with Fiona Gilchrist.

1975	M Moir and J Ramsay
1976	M M Dalgleish and E Belch
1977	M J Plenderleath and F Gilchrist
1978	L Morrison and A Palmer
1979	M Moir and J Ramsay
1980	M J Plenderleath and F Gilchrist
1981	F Gilchrist and M Plenderleath
1982	F Scott and B Gilchrist
1983	L McAuley and D Robertson
1984	E Belch and A Van Der Lee
1985	B Scougall and M Dalgleish
1986	M Moir and J Ramsay
1987	M Dalgleish and B Scougall
1988	A Johnstone and M Carlaw
1989	J Coubrough and J Mill
1990	P Elliott and K Rogers
1991	A Halligan and V Dykes
1992	F Gilchrist and M Plenderleath

FROSTBITE GREENSOMES CUP

Jean Ramsay presented this cup after her term as captain, and is a matchplay competition held between October and March with all rounds played over 11 holes except for the final which is a full round. Like Morag Plenderleath, Jean has appeared reluctant at times to allow others custody of the silverware having won it no fewer than six times and is the current holder along with Anne Carswell.

1978	E Bush and B Scougall
1979	D Robertson and A Prime
1980	M Dalgleish and A Prime
1981	M Moir and M Leaf
1982	J Mill and A Halligan
1983	J Ramsay and V McIntyre
1984	E Belch and J Ramsay
1985	J Mill and B Scougall
1986	E Bush and A Prime
1987	J Ramsay and A Halligan
1988	A Halligan and J Mill
1989	M Moir and J Ramsay
1990	P Elliott and M Frew
1991	J Ramsay and A Carswell
1992	A Carswell and J Ramsay

NORAH MILLER SENIOR TROPHY

This trophy was presented by Norah Miller, wife of Alistair, a past president and captain, who once held or shared the gent's course record. Entry is restricted to over-55s. Two rounds are played usually in conjunction with a medal, and the better 18-hole net score is chosen to determine the winner.

1981	V McIntyre	1987	M Dalgleish
1982	J Coubrough	1988	E Hamilton
1983	M Walker	1989	M Dalgleish
1984	M Jeffrey	1990	J Mill
1985	E Hamilton	1991	J Coubrough
1986	B Scougall	1992	F Gilchrist

BRONZE CHAMPIONSHIP CUP

This is played for in the same way as the Ladies

Championship except it is for those in the higher handicap range, and was presented by former captain Fiona Gilchrist, whose family has had connections with the club over four generations. In the 1920's, Fiona's grandmother, Mrs. E Elderton, was lady captain plus captain of Dumbarton County. Her mother, Mrs. W McKenzie, was a committee member and her daughter, Barbara Kettlewell was match secretary before moving to Dunblane with her family in the 1980's.

1974 D M Lawson	1984 F Fox
1975 N M Miller	1985 M Carlaw
1976 S A Reid	1986 B McDonald
1977 J R Rankin	1987 J Mill
1978 R Doran	1988 A Mackay
1979 A Prime	1989 A Johnstone
1980 A Halligan	1990 A Johnstone
1981 J Mill	1991 V Dykes
1982 A Mackay	1992 V Dykes
1983 R Doran	

NEILSON CUP

This trophy was presented by Mrs Hugh Neilson for ringer competition in 1949 and is in aid of Red Cross. The format is that entrants submit a card any time between April and September and thereafter improved scores either in medals or in day cards at individual holes are ringed. It is similar to an eclectic, except that once a score has been ringed no further improvements are allowed.

1949 M D Forsyth	1971 J Ramsay
1950 C Lennie	1972 M Plenderleath
1951 M D Forsyth	1973 P L McAuley
1952 M D Forsyth	1974 A Reece
1953 E E Stanton	1975 F Gilchrist
1954 J Auld and G U Laird	1976 L McCathie
1955 J Auld and M D Forsyth	1977 P L McAuley
1956 M J Stewart	1978 F Gilchrist
1957 M J Stewart	1979 M Moir
1958 M D Forsyth	1980 L McAuley
1959 A Reece	1981 M Moir
1960 A Reece	1982 L McCathie
1961 A Reece	1983 F Gilchrist
1962 A Reece	1984 F Gilchrist
1963 A Reece	1985 M Moir
1964 A Reece	1986 F Scott
1965 N M Miller	1987 M Calaw
1966 N M Miller	1988 S Reid
1967 A Reece	1989 F Gilchrist
1968 A Reece and B Cameron	1990 F Gilchrist
1969 J R Rankin	1991 A Halligan
1970 A Reece	1992 F Gilchrist

MRS WELWISHERS CUP

Anonymously donated, this is a ringer competition like the Neilson Cup only for bronze players. The apparent mis-spelling in the name of the trophy is thought to be an engraver's error.

1984 E Hamilton	1989 A Mackay
1985 J Cairns	1990 J Coubrough
1986 J Coubrough	1991 C Perella
1987 J Brown	1992 M Rice
1988 J Brown	

CHALLENGE SHIELD

This matchplay competition is restricted to players with handicaps of 36 or no handicap and was introduced to encourage new members. A rule introduced in recent years is that if a player has her handicap reduced in the course of the competition she must concede strokes to her opponent.

Anne Carswell did so in 1990, carding a medal score of net 59 which identified her as a Glasgow Herald club golf bandit of the week and qualified her for the Parbusters final at Haggs Castle which she duly won.

1981 A Trainer	1987 P Price
1982 D Shirra	1988 M Barrowman
1983 E Twitchings	1989 A Carswell
1984 M Petrie	1990 A Carswell
1985 C Smart	1991 C Henderson
1986 P Bruce	1992 C Henderson

CAPTAIN'S CUP

This is an 18-hole medal competition played in June, on Lady Captain's Day, and was presented by Vera McIntyre at the end of her term of captaincy.

1982 S Reid	1988 F Gilchrist
1983 S Reid	1989 M Dalgleish
1984 F Fox	1990 A Carswell
1985 M Carlaw	1991 P Elliot
1986 F Hardie	1992 B Houston
1987 A Johnstone	

DOROTHY LAWSON TROPHY

This is the fourball championship and the trophy was presented by Dr. John Lawson in memory of his wife who was vice-captain at the time of her death.

1975	D E Robertson and M M Dalgleish
1976	M Moir and D Stirton
1977	D E Robertson and M M Dalgleish
1978	L McCathie and M Moir
1979	L McCathie and M Moir
1980	F Gilchrist and J Ramsay
1981	M Moir and A Prime
1982	M Moir and A Prime
1983	M Moir and A Prime
1984	M Dalgleish and R Doran
1985	M Moir and A Prime
1986	A Halligan and F Hardie
1987	K Black and C Smart
1988	A Mackay and S Reid
1989	D Robertson and M Belch
1990	K Rogers and J Horan
1991	M Spence and F Scott
1992	M Moir and A Prime

MARGARET MEGAW TROPHY

This is a three-round eclectic competition and was presented by Mr. Megaw in memory of his wife. Proceeds from the entry money for this competition are donated each year to Cancer Research.

1987	F Gilchrist	1990	F Gilchrist
1988	M Moir	1991	C Craig
1989	F Gilchrist	1992	M Rice

MILNE CENTENARY TROPHY

This is the Open Day trophy, presented by J Milne, and began life as a foursome competition but has since been altered, because of the falling number of entrants, to individual medal play.

1984	A Prime and S Reid, Helensburgh
1986	J MacPherson and I Ferguson, Helensburgh
1987	J Gardner and I Rose, Haggs Castle
1988	I Shannon and N Frame, Dunblane and Alloa
1989	B McDonald and A Mackay, Helensburgh
1990	B Scougall, Helensburgh
1991	M H Rice, Helensburgh
1992	M H Rice, Helensburgh

BEN BOUIE TROPHY

The current annual open mixed foursomes competition for the Ben Bouie Trophy, presented by former captain Dr. Ellis Belch and husband Jim, started in 1985 and an average of 100 couples have entered each year.

Mixed play has a long history at Helensburgh and the earliest record was in September 1901. The prizes of a set of silver brushes for the first lady and silver hair ornaments for the runner-up were presented by the Misses Stevens and Applegarth.

1985	Mr J Harper and Mrs B Harper, Cardross
1986	Mr A Lawson and Miss D Shirra, Helensburgh
1987	Mr V McLaren and Miss D Macrae, Campsie
1988	Mr A W Frew and Mrs M Frew, Helensburgh
1989	Mr and Mrs Montgomerie, Greenock
1990	Mr W Fleming and Mrs J Brown, Dullatur
1991	Mr A Miller and Mrs J Coubrough
1992	Mr J Munro and Mrs M Spence

ARDMORE TROPHY

Presented by Fred and Ann Prime to the best Helensburgh couple in the Helensburgh Mixed Open Foursomes.

1987	Katherine Black and David Griffiths
1988	Bill and Betty Hill
1989	Les and Rosemary Cox
1990	Moira Spence and John Munro
1991	Jessie Coubrough and Alex Miller
1992	John Munro and Moira Spence

DORMAY CUP

This is a ladies and juniors competition and the name has nothing to do with being so many holes up with that number of holes to play. It was presented by Dorothy Robertson (the Dor bit) and May Dalgleish (the may bit) at a time when they had four and two sons respectively, playing junior golf.

The format is greensome which invariably puts the juniors under pressure on the tee, as none of them like to have their dignity hurt by being outdriven by a lady.

1974	D Stirton and I Miller
1975	A Maynard and D Kirk
1976	J Rankin and B Mill
1977	L McCathie and R Elder
1978	K M Black and B Mill
1979	G Schofield and R Elder
1980	L Petrie and G Belch
1981	G Nuttall and A Brown
1982	M Plenderleath and S Clark
1983	J Cairns and M McKenzie
1984	A MacKay S Gethin
1985	F Gilchrist and G Barrowman
1986	E Armstrong and S Gethin
1987	D Robertson and G S Nicol
1988	K M Black and A B Martin

1989   C Perella and J N Latham
1990   C Annesley and J N Latham
1991   M Rice and J N Latham
1992   S Reid and A Sharpe

HALLIGAN PUTTER

In 1988, Alisoun Halligan presented this hickory putter to be played for annually at the Ladies v Gents match. After five years of very close matches, the honours list reads two victories for the men, one for the ladies and two draws. The putter originally belonged to Alisoun's mother, who had a handicap of 1 and was a past lady captain of Ranfurly Castle and Renfrewshire Ladies Golfing Association.

JUNIOR TROPHIES

STUART F JEFFREY AND JOHN M HARPER MEMORIAL TROPHY

This fine silver trophy was presented to the club as a tribute to the memory of two talented young members who died in a tragic motoring accident in 1980 and is awarded each year to the winner of the junior club championship.

The current holder is James Latham, the 1992 junior captain, and while several boys have won the trophy more than once it is unlikely anyone will equal the feat of Gary Orr who took the title four years in a row.

1973 C Ferguson	1983 G Orr
1974 C Dalgleish	1984 G Orr
1975 C Dalgleish	1985 G Orr
1976 C Dalgleish	1986 C Reid
1977 G Dalgleish	1987 N Fortune
1978 G Dalgleish	1988 S Graham
1979 D Stewart	1989 S Graham
1980 T Reid	1990 N Fortune
1981 A Fraser	1991 S Graham
1982 G Orr	1992 J Latham

PAUL CHALLENGE MEDAL

The Paul Medal is the oldest junior trophy in the club, dating back to 1907 when it was won for the first time by a young man with the grandiose name of Harrington Robley. Since then it has been contested on no fewer than 76 occasions (the competition was suspended during the Second World War) and a study of the list of winners would provide older members with an interesting walk down memory lane.

The medal was presented to the junior section by a distinguished member of that time, Harry S Paul, who was a driving force behind the move to increase the course from 9 to 18 holes, and was the course architect. The medal was won in 1913 by Master H L Paul, presumably a son or even a grandson of the benefactor. A more recent winner, Master Evan McGregor (1957) can still occasionally put together a good round.

Colin Dalgleish, currently club champion and captain-elect of the Scottish amateur team, won the medal in 1974 and again in 1976 in preparation for his subsequent successful assault on the National Championship in 1981 and a Walker Cup place.

1907 H Robley	1954 K Craig
1908 T L Burnside	1955 I M Still
1909 T L Burnside	1956 K Craig
1910 T L Burnside	1957 E McGregor
1911 C H Robley	1958 D Butler
1912 K A McKenzie	1959 D Butler
1913 H L Paul	1960 R McLean
1914 A M Duncan	1961 A Smith
1915 E W McCormick	1962 A Smith
1916 I H McKenzie	1963 W E Walker
1917 A H Paterson	1964 H S Thomson
1918 N A W Robinson	1965 D J Amy
1919 J L McFadyen	1966 J D C Mackay
1920 L G Whyte	1967 J D C Mackay
1921 J M Gray	1968 J W Findlay
1922 L G Whyte	1969 A J Lawson
1923 S T Pigott	1970 R Clark
1924 E R Herbertson	1971 S Kirk
1925 S T Pigott	1972 G McAuley
1926 A G Miller	1973 J Harper
1928 E R Herbertson	1974 C Dalgleish
1929 C R Steven	1975 D Park
1930 R B F Wylie	1976 C Dalgleish
1931 J C P Sloan	1977 J Friel
1932 G M Milne	1978 J M Graham
1933 R B Laing	1979 D Miller
1934 R Aitkenhead	1980 C Cameron
1935 D C Weir	1981 G Craig
1936 W A Strain	1982 G Miller
1937 J H Weir	1983 C Woess
1938 T B Henderson	1984 A Morton
1939 W Aitkenhead	1985 C Reid
1947 I Campbell	1986 C Reid
1948 M Rafferty	1988 M Folland
1949 R M Still	1989 S Gethin
1950 A J Green	1990 S Barclay
1951 C Lyon Jr	1991 S Barclay
1952 G Niven	1992 R Makeham
1953 I M Still	

NB: No winner is recorded against years 1927, 1940 to 1946 inclusive and 1987.

SINCLAIR MACKAY CUP

Not as old as the Paul Medal but none the less dating back more than 40 years the Sinclair Mackay Cup was first contested in 1951 when the winner was Master Gordon Burgess, better known now for his painting than his putting. It is a handicap competition played in the singles matchplay format and there are 42 names on the trophy. Many of the early winners are as well known and as active as the more recent ones.

Sinclair Mackay, who is in the photograph of members of "The Tin House Club" in Chapter 3, was a superintendent with the Dunbartonshire Police, a secretary of the Scottish Police Golf Association and a keen supporter of junior golf.

1951	J G Burgess	1972	S Kirk
1952	J Spy Jr	1973	J Miller
1953	I M Still	1974	J Miller
1954	I M Still	1975	B Robertson
1955	I M Still	1976	G Dalgleish
1956	W Thornton	1977	R Elder
1957	W Thornton	1978	D Stewart
1958	D Butler	1979	T Reid
1959	D Butler	1980	E McLean
1960	I T Rankine	1981	A Fraser
1961	J Fairlie	1982	J Graham
1962	A Smith	1983	S Barlass
1963	J S G Lennox	1984	K Reid
1964	J S G Lennox	1985	S Farrow
1965	R J Amy	1986	C Reid
1966	J D C McKay	1987	G McKay
1967	J S G Lennox	1988	S Barclay
1968	D W Weir	1989	S Gethin
1969	D W Weir	1990	S Barclay
1970	A J Lawson	1991	B Nichol
1971	N S Addison	1992	S Towler

CRAIG CUP

Presented by Joe Craig, then junior convener and later to become club captain in 1990/91, the Craig Cup was first contested in 1979 and is a foursomes matchplay competition.

1979	E McLean and G A Belch
1980	T Reid and D Stewart
1981	D Stewart and T Reid
1982	G Miller and A Brown
1983	C McKenzie and C Reid
1984	C McKenzie and C Reid
1985	M Kelly and S Farrow
1986	S Gethin and G S Nicol
1987	C Reid and G McKay
1988	B Halligan and S Kelly
1989	S Graham and S Barclay
1990	S Gill and J Cleland
1991	M Currie and B Nichol
1992	A Currie and A Sinclair

FORELAND BOWL

First contested in 1975 the format of the competition for the Foreland Bowl is fourball matchplay.

The silver bowl was presented by Douglas and May Dalgleish, and called after the name of their house located opposite the clubhouse at a time when their sons Colin and Gordon were in an emerging junior section which was in need of more competitions and silverware.

1975	B Robertson and J McAuley
1976	G Dalgleish and J Harper
1977	G Dalgleish and J Harper
1978	D Stewart and A Robertson
1979	R Elder and C McKillop
1980	C Cameron and M Fraser
1981	J Graham and C McGibbon
1982	K Reid and G Orr
1983	S Woess and S Barlass
1984	G Nicol and J Redpath
1985	N Fortune and S Graham
1986	S Farrow and M Kelly
1987	M Kelly and S Farrow
1988	M Folland and S Westwell
1989	N Fortune and C Woess
1990	A Currie and J Darroch
1991	Not concluded
1992	I Crawford and P Pullar

McKINNON STILL TROPHY (Captain's Cup)

Presented by Mr. Ian McKinnon Still, a former club champion, this silver cup is awarded to the winner of the captain's prize, an 18 hole medal competition (handicap) which is played towards the end of the season.

1981	Kenneth Reid	1986	C Reid
1982	J Graham	1987/9	No winners
1983	S Woess	1990	J Darroch
1984	K Reid	1991	A Overend
1985	M Kelly	1992	S Towler

THE EAGLE TANKARD

Contrary to popular belief the name of this trophy is not derived from a golfing feat which few of us achieve in a lifetime of trying. In fact the only relevance it has to golf is the donor, Gordon Dalgleish, whose name appears on at least three of the aforementioned trophies.

It appears Gordon was en route from Southampton to Lisbon on a vessel bearing the name MV Eagle when he was tempted to try his luck in a simulated horse race and won the tankard which was then presented to him by Michael Parkinson. Too young to use it for its intended purpose he very generously donated it to the junior section.

A special competition was introduced in 1974 for boys with handicaps above 18 and this took the form of singles matchplay contested by eight qualifiers from two medal rounds.

1974 D Stewart	1984 R Morrison
1975 W Petrie	1985 A Martin
1976 J Percy	1986 S Gethin
1977 A Fraser	1987 M Kelly
1978 J Friel	1988 R McDonald
1979 R Elder	1989 R Curtis
1980 G Orr	1990 A McFarlane
1981 K Reid	1991 A Currie
1982 C Reid	1992 A Sinclair
1983 R Morrison	

SUMMER CHAMPIONSHIP TROPHY

Donated by Ian Stewart and first contested in 1975, the trophy is awarded to the boy achieving the best handicap performance in the Summer Championship Series.

1975 R Hunter	1984 J Redpath
1976 J Graham	1985 R J Coats
1977 A Fraser	1986 S Gethin
1978 A Fraser	1987 G Nicol
1979 A M Robertson	1988 C Donald
1980 J McCallum	1989 S Barclay
1981 J McBlane	1990 I Crawford
1982 C McKenzie	1991 W Ritchie
1983 J Redpath	1992 G Parker

JUNIOR OUTING TROPHY

Donated by two club members, the trophy is a Shield which is contested during the annual outing over 36 holes Stableford.

1989 J Cleland (Palacerigg)	1991 M Currie (Palacerigg)
1990 S Gill (Greenock)	1992 A Sinclair (Stirling)

SUMMER CUP

Presented by Dick Sawkins on behalf of Atlantic Research Corporation and Gareloch Engineering this trophy is contested over a series of six medal rounds played during the school summer holiday period. The winner is the boy with the lowest aggregate for his three best scratch scores of the series.

1989 R Curtis	1991 S Graham
1990 S Graham	1992 R Makeham

FESTIVAL OF GOLF WEEK COMPETITIONS

HELENSBURGH BOYS OPEN

Introduced in 1976 the Helensburgh Boys Open, sponsored by AGGREKO and played during the Festival of Golf Week every July, has become one of the highlights of the Scottish Junior Golfing Calendar, attracting entries from a wide area.

Two qualifying medal rounds are followed by matchplay rounds culminating in the final on the Saturday of Festival Week. The lowest eight non-qualifiers contest a separate matchplay competition for which a Silver Flight Trophy is awarded.

Helensburgh Golf Club's Festival of Golf Week was initiated in 1976 by Ian Stewart, the then match and handicap secretary, encompassing the open Craig Orr Trophy gents foursomes competition and adding other events to involve the entire membership.

Initially the open boys competition was simply a small part of the festival, but it quickly developed into the main event.

Its status was enhanced by its inclusion in the Royal Bank of Scotland Merit Award scheme with a ranking just below that of the Scottish Boys Championship. This was achieved by persuading Scottish Golf Union officials, notably Sandy Sinclair and the late Jack Wallace, that the presence of leading overseas juniors, attracted to the tournament through the Dalgleish family contact with the International Junior Masters tournament at East Aurora, in Buffalo, USA, enhanced the value of the Helensburgh event.

Several of the winners have gone on to greater things. Gary Orr's exploits are detailed in Chapter 4 and those of Colin Dalgleish in Chapter 5. Of the others Adam Hunter has gone on to become an established European Tour player, while Mark Brennan is the professional at Campsie, Euan McIntosh, based at Turnhouse, won the Tartan Tour's 1992 assistant's order of merit, and Ross Aitken is an assistant to Bill Lockie at Kilmarnock Barassie.

1976	A Waddington, Bothwell Castle	
1977	J H Anderson, East Renfrewshire	
1978	C R Dalgleish, Helensburgh	
1979	G D McNab, Alloa	
1980	A Hunter, Sandyhills	
1981	G Johnstone, Greenburn	
1982	A Turnbull, Peebles	
1983	M J Brennan, Easter Moffat	
1984	G Orr, Helensburgh	
1985	E McIntosh, Turnhouse	
1986	G R Aitken, Largs	
1987	S Duffy, Shotts	
1988	A Weir, Hilton Park	
1989	C Dun, Torwoodlee	
1990	L W Kelly, Cowal	
1991	G MacFarlane, Clydebank & District	
1992	D M Campbell, Machrihanish	

DOUGLAS B LOWE MEMORIAL TROPHY

This trophy dedicated to the memory of a popular past captain, who died suddenly in the clubhouse in 1978, is awarded to the boy aged not more than 16 who achieves the best performance in the Helensburgh Boys Open.

Douglas Lowe, born in Arbroath, was a well-known personality in the fifties and sixties through his radio football commentaries and came to Helensburgh in 1963 when he was appointed head of public relations at BBC Scotland.

He is well remembered as a competitive left-hander on the course and a raconteur of note in the clubhouse. His term of captaincy was, in reality, one year more than that with which he is credited, having as vice captain assumed the senior role during the second year of office of his predecessor Leslie Bamford who left the area.

1979	R Hamilton, Kirkhill
1980	A J Hamilton, Sandyhills
1981	M Campbell, Muckhart
1982	A Turnbull, Peebles
1983	M J Brennan, Easter Moffat
1984	F O'Callaghan, Haggs Castle
1985	E McIntosh, Turnhouse
1986	G R Aitken, Largs
1987	S Duffy, Shotts
1988	M Brooks, Carluke
1989	Craig Dun, Torwoodlee
1990	Lorne W Kelly, Cowal
1991	G MacFarlane, Clydebank & District
1992	J Cleland, Helensburgh

CORNELIUS MUNDIE TROPHY

Presented by Cornelius Mundie, a well known Helensburgh businessman, this trophy is for the best performance in the Helensburgh Boys Open by a local junior.

1988 S Gethin	1991 J Latham
1989 S Graham	1992 J Cleland
1990 No winner	

MIDWAY TROPHY

This was presented by the festival committee for an Open Stableford competition midway through the week.

1981 P Quinn	1987 F F Currie
1982 R Stocker	1988 W Hill
1983 T A D Reid	1989 A Hurst
1984 R C Doig	1990 H Parker
1985 E McGregor	1991 J Main
1986 E McGregor	1992 P Jackson

CRAIG ORR CUP

This was presented in 1968 by Craig Rankine and J P Orr Erskine for the winning pair in the gents open foursomes competition which nowadays is the pipe-opener to the Festival of Golf Week. With few exceptions Helensburgh pairs have won the trophy and now collect with it the W S McNeil Trophy for the best local score.

1968	J P O Erskine and D C T Rankin
1969	J Orr and W Thornton
1970	J Dow and J Powell
1971	F Shields and T Griffiths
1972	D E Carswell and R Winning
1973	M Kelly and J Fenton
1974	R Greer and J Paton
1975	R McGregor and P English
1976	G B Nicol and G K Jack
1977	J M Graham and R S D Howarth
1978	D Robertson and J A McAuley
1979	A Barnes and W Bell
1980	H I McDonald and I Brown
1981	E H McGregor and J Munro
1982	G Perella and G Orr
1983	J Riddle and S Coutts
1984	R Burns and N Prime
1985	D Holms and A Glass
1986	M D Scougall and A W Fraser
1987	E Fraser and D Baxter
1988	D G Beattie and G W Beattie
1989	W McLean and C Ralph

1990	G P Mickel and A Latham
1991	E McGregor and F Platt
1992	L Munro and R McLean

W S McNEIL TROPHY

This trophy was presented by Mrs McNeil in memory of Stewart, a low handicap player for many years. The chosen use was for the best Helensburgh pair in the open foursomes strokeplay competition. Today the open foursomes marks the start of the Festival of Golf Week which coincides with the last day of the Open Championship. There was, however, a ruling in the first year which restricted one pair to one prize and the winners ought to have been Messrs. Carswell and Winning who had the overall best score for the Craig Orr Cup but the next Helensburgh pair were awarded the W S McNeil Trophy. Despite this, it does seem fitting that Munro and McGregor were the beneficiaries.

1972	J Munro and E H McGregor
1973	W S Gilchrist and K McDougall
1974	D Griffiths and R Smith
1976	G Beattie and I McDonald
1977	C G Sinclair and P B Reece
1978	D Griffiths and R Smith
1979	A M Robertson and J Harper
1980	A M Robertson and A D Fraser
1981	J Munro and E H McGregor
1982	G Perella and G Orr
1983	P K Mill and B R Mill
1984	R Burns and N Prime
1985	W Trail and W Petrie
1986	M D Scougall and A W Fraser
1987	E Fraser and D Baxter
1988	D G Beattie and G W Beattie
1989	W McLean and C Ralph
1990	G P Mickel and A Latham
1991	E McGregor and F Platt
1992	L Munro and R McLean

HERON CUP

This trophy was presented by J Urquhart Heron in 1981 for annual open competition at Helensburgh by seniors, the donor winning his own prize in the second year of competition. The winners below are Helensburgh members unless stated.

1981	R Tough, Clydebank & District	1987	R Ralph
1982	J Urquhart Heron	1988	R Ralph
1983	T Adair	1989	H McPherson
1984	B G Samuels, Bonnyton	1990	D S Baxter
1985	P J Jackson	1991	D S Baxter
1986	A W Fraser	1992	J Doran

The golf festival also includes a gents handicap matchplay tournament, for which there is a pre-qualifying medal round. There is at least one fun evening on the Thursday, when Helensburgh plays the Peninsula for the PenHelen Trophy. Qualifications for membership of the respective teams are at best obscure. The Peninsula appears to embrace unlikely places such as Cardross, with the team captain now based in Govan. The selection process exhibits clique tendencies.

There are traditional captain and vice captain days dating back to 1894, with special prizes and hospitality, much enjoyed by the members. Various captains and vice captains have endeavoured to enhance these days, which have tended to become obscured by the plethora of competitions presently available. There were also a number of special competitions held during the Second World War in aid of charity. Various other competitions arise from time to time, mainly through sponsorship and special promotions by companies which are most welcome. We mention only a few in this book, but acknowledge the important part played by all sponsors, in their support of a wide variety of events, including normal monthly medals. A number of sponsors will feature strongly in centenary year.

WINTER GOLF

For many years there have been competitions during the winter months. There is even reference to winter foursomes in 1912. Winter leagues do seem to be modern inventions and a number of variations have been tried. A few years ago, Brunton Miller (which means John Steele, Douglas Dalgleish and other unwitting partners) decided to adopt what has turned out to be a most popular event.

The 1992 version has 144 gents, plus a queue of reserves, taking part in this fourball, better ball, Stableford, team, pair and eclectic competition. The organisers even rejected the vice captain's late entry of another team. Handicaps are savaged during the winter league on a temporary basis.

Some have in the past objected to the hogging of tee times but many have now joined in the fun, which lasts for eight weeks from mid October, culminating in a dinner in December. The ladies are allowed their own modest version.

Thereafter, one hopes that the course is rested, in keeping with Old Tom's wish for nae Sunday play but forlorn is a word which comes to mind.

INTER-CLUB MATCHES

The longest running event is the 20-a-side game between Helensburgh and Cardross which dates back at least to 1930. The original format was annually home and away but in recent years the venue has alternated. It seems clear that the game has always been a sociable one although the results were minuted at one time. Nowadays the official result is invariably a draw.

Sadly the match has almost foundered on apathy, although not from Helensburgh's viewpoint. Given the foundation of a team comprising committee plus a selection of others, from time to time there has been some petulance when newcomers were allowed in. Maybe there ought to be a modest trophy to provide a focus.

In the late 1960s, the late Douglas Lowe was one of the founders of an annual home-and-away match against Cowal. On most occasions the method of transport was by boat between Helensburgh and Dunoon.

Usually the outward journey was routine but return trips yielded some exciting experiences and one or two near drownings. One incident involved a Helensburgh player who, carefully negotiating the pier steps with clubs on shoulder, contrived to empty the entire set into 20 feet of water.

As befitting perfect hosts, Cowal members retrieved the clubs the following day at low tide and arranged for their safe return to Helensburgh.

Another member, joining in a bit of fun while waiting for the boat by hitting new golf balls from the pier into the Clyde, later discovered to his chagrin that the ammunition had come from his own bag.

For a time the outing was over-subscribed and one year a second team made their own arrangements. Eventually the Helensburgh view was that Cowal were

The contestants of a Helensburgh v Cardross match in the 1970s, many of whom remain weel kent faces today.

mutating the game into a serious low-handicap team event and so it faded away and was discontinued.

In 1978, Jim Stark was captain of Helensburgh and his office colleague Bill McMillan was captain of Kilmarnock Barassie. As a result an inter-committee, home-and-away match ensued. The match has since developed into a clique event with office bearers and committee members rarely featuring on either side. There is a trophy known as the Deknockhellcanter which serves a useful purpose at lunch and dinner as the port is passed around. Golf, incidentally, does feature as well.

In one of the early matches, Stark and Tom Griffiths were playing Alan Stewart and Jim Brown, the former Kilmarnock and Hearts goalkeeper. On the fifth tee at Barassie with the wind from 10 o'clock, Brown commented that this was the hardest par 4 in the west. Wishing to remain anonymous today, Griffiths' partner, receiving a stroke, then achieved the equivalent of a 30-yard shot past the goalie into the postage stamp corner by holing a No.3 iron shot for a two net one.

Recently Pat Mundie and Jim Barrowman have been instrumental in creating two new inter-club ventures against Buchanan Castle and Cathkin Braes. The Buchanan match has an official aura, the participants mainly being from the respective committees, while the Cathkin version is undoubtedly, at this time, in the clique category. Both matches are in their formative years.

It was discovered in 1992 at Barassie that there is a Barassie-Cathkin Braes association which goes back 50 years. Perhaps there are the makings of a triangular fixture.

In the ladies section there are early records of games against Douglas Park, Bearsden, Kilmacolm, Greenock and Bogside, Skelmorlie, Drumchapel, Dumbarton and Cardross.

Colourful occasions they seem to have been too because, with the exception of the matches that obviously involved boat trips, the ladies were driven to away fixtures by a chauffeur called McFarlane who invariably wore a peaked cap and leather breeches, and also caddied. The ladies, in turn, always wore hats, even when playing.

In 1913, for a year until the outbreak of the First World War and resuming in 1921, the arrangements were more regulated and Helensburgh ladies joined the West of Scotland League and played against Cardross, Greenock, Kilmacolm and Bridge of Weir.

CHAPTER 9

Course guide

DELIGHTS GALORE FOR RABBITS AND TIGERS ALIKE

WHEN all is said and done, playing the golf course is what the club is about and doing so within and occasionally better than our own limits and expectations. Hope springs eternal and the next time we do so we unfailingly believe that this could be the round of a lifetime even though we may have had no more than a couple of practice swishes and therefore no logical reason to think the performance will be better than the usual display of unmitigated incompetence.

The holes until 1970 were, as far as we are aware, nameless but the committee of the day, under the captaincy of Douglas Lowe, decided to change this in consultation with the members who were invited to make suggestions.

Some were taken up and others rejected, and one in the latter category was the 15th, where the Churchill Estate providing quarters for servicemen based at the Clyde Submarine Base and their families had come into being within easy striking distance of a moderate slice.

The suggestion of calling this hole "Balls to the Navy" was considered apt in one sense and hilariously rude in the other. In the end the more prosaic and less offensive "Churchill" was plumped for.

Dispatching "balls to the navy" still occurs despite a message pinned to the notice board at one point which probably made matters worse by planting the dreaded thought firmly in the mind of all members and which read: "Would members please try not to hit ball into the Churchill Estate."

The latest attempt to end this danger is more than a thought being planted, it is several hundred fir trees which, when they mature, will certainly lessen the hazard but surely never remove it. The incompetence of the average golfer will ensure that.

All the names, detailed below, are self-explanatory except for the 14th "Baillie's Brig" which refers to the one-time bridge spanning the dry gully and in use for many years at both the 14th and 17th. It was the cause celebre of the then captain John Baillie, but sadly the bridge was subject to vandalism, fell into disrepair and was eventually removed.

There follows two course guides, one the way we would like to play, denoted by the Tiger Route, and other the harsh reality, which we call the Rabbit Route. The first is a figment of our imagination and the latter comes courtesy of John Rees, whose ability, it must be said, is better than he professes if only marginally, and stems from a speech he made at a winter league dinner, making the point that those who go round in level par miss so many of the delightful nature rambles discovered by the high-handicapper, who learns to regard the ball almost as a friendly guide to the countryside. He tells us:

"I have been persuaded to reveal my golf secret which cannot fail to help you break the 100 barrier. At this level, yardages and club selection are meaningless and in this system length is denoted by the number of practice swings (PS) and degree of difficulty by the number of waggles (W), for example the ninth, crossing the Old Luss Road, is PS1 and W 10.

Pick your own route then, and let's tee off.

1 High Hopes. 283 yards. Par 4. Stroke index 13.
Tiger: A good tee shot, with a long iron or short wood and a pitch on to the green sloping back towards the tee will provide a birdie opportunity. Big hitters might consider driving the green and going for an eagle, but bunkers short of the green and to the right and left are very much in play.

Rabbit: (PS 2, W10). The extreme degree of difficulty is due to the pitying glance of the starter. Bunkers on the right belong to the Tom Morris era of guttie balls but can easily be found with a high-tech boron-shafted club, though this is due, in part, to the club itself. This is preferable, however, to a lost ball out of bounds on the left. A rebound from the tree on the right, or the fence on the left, is a consideration, and one once

	WHITE	YELLOW	RED	
1 YDS	283	262	263	HIGH HOPES
PAR	4	4	4	
SI	13	13	11	

	WHITE	YELLOW	RED	
2 YDS	429	402	395	FRUIN
PAR	4	4	5	
SI	3	3	1	

	WHITE	YELLOW	RED	
3 YDS	182	151	147	MIRROR OF THE MOOR
PAR	3	3	3	
SI	11	11	15	

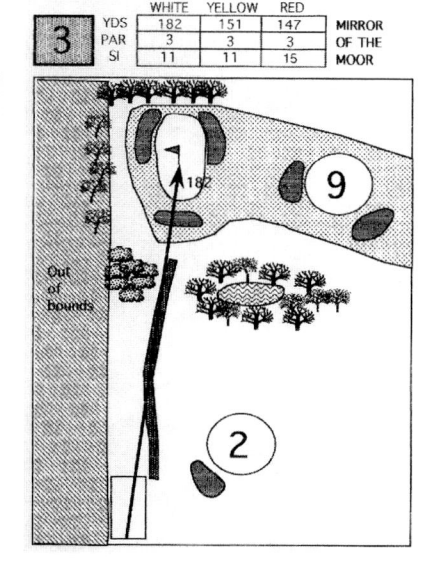

stopped nine inches from the pin on the 18th. It was tapped in a for a course record of 2, immediately celebrated in the bar.

2   Fruin. 429 yards. Par 4. Stroke index 3.

Tiger: Although the second longest par 4, a long iron is a wise choice of club to avoid finishing partly up a hill just over 200 yards away. That will leave a level stance for another long iron or spoon shot for the blind second. Finding the green in two shots is good play here even for a tiger.

Rabbit: (PS 8, W 4). The long trolley haul gives ample time to dread this tee, hemmed in by trees and with out of bounds on the left. The main terror is the bunker at the top of the hill. A No.8 iron should be chosen, on the second, third or even fourth (any more offers?) to pass it. The proposed new tee is nearer the fence and has a longer carry. Are there vacancies at Cardross?

3   Mirror of the Moor. 182 yards. Par 3. Stroke index 3.

Tiger: Check the wind as your club selection could be anything from a No.7 iron to a No.3 wood. That's all there is to it as, with a slight draw, you fly the ball over the trees surrounding what is left of the pond that gave the hole its name. The green slopes from back to front and helps stop the ball.

Rabbit: (PS 2, W8). Yoga practitioners can blot out the out of bounds on the left, trees and frog spawn for this superb test of half-warm, untrained muscles.

A 4 may be achieved by playing for the 9th green. Beware of the distracting "uproar of butterflies," as P G Wodehouse would say, in the adjoining field. Twelve shots would not be a record here.

4   Ben Bouie. 372 yards. Par 4. Stroke index 7.

Tiger: Against a backdrop of the ben, a drive down two slopes will leave a short-iron approach to the slightly elevated green, employing backspin to prevent the ball running through. A reasonable birdie chance.

Rabbit: (PS 3, W 2). A straightforward relief after the third, especially since a kindly greens manager has drawn the teeth of "Jaws" recently. The winter green is harder than the normal one, curiously. Cutting the new trees back to 5ft 11 ins and staking them would be a kindness to high handicappers.

5   Bunker Hill. 260 yards. Par 4. Stroke index 15.

Tiger: The green at the top of the hill is driveable, but a little course management is advisable. It is wiser to lay up or be pin high right leaving a simple pitch and single putt. Taking 4 here is really a dropped shot.

Rabbit: (PS 2, W 4). Senior members should invest in the new Mark III pacemaker (the five-speed model) before tackling this one. A drive which rolls back to the bottom is depressing, but at least Jaws II has been provided with a drawbridge. Don't expect any help from the handicap unless receiving 15 strokes. Players are advised not to talk and smoke during this hole - the health authority has only one four-wheel-drive ambulance on call, usually parked at Vale of Leven.

6   Loch Lomond. 412 yards. Par 4. Stroke index 5.

Tiger: The classic way to play the hole is not to cut the corner - that's for gorillas. Instead, shape the shot for the hole and draw the ball round the corner to leave a short iron approach landing directly on the green to avoid unpredictable bounces. This tactic will present a good birdie chance.

Rabbit: (PS 6, W 6) A local entrepreneur might profit from Moor Balls concessions. Beware also of water blisters on the fairway - one could be lost without trace. Our joy at finding no bunkers is tempered by greater terrors than its delightful name suggests - there is a view over the southern reaches of the loch and it's a great hole to lift your head. Avoid during north east gales. It's a long way to the bar.

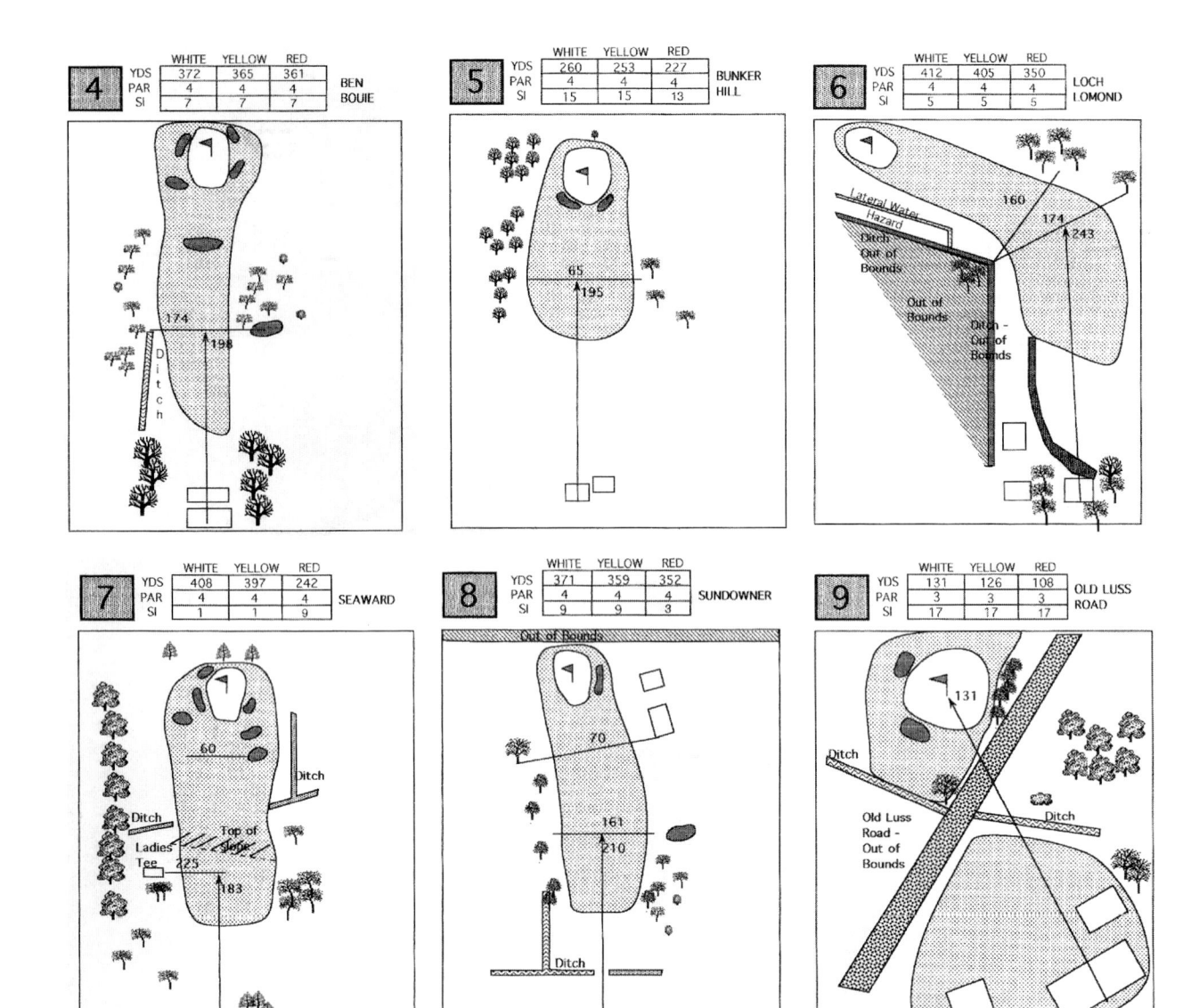

4		WHITE	YELLOW	RED	
	YDS	372	365	361	BEN
	PAR	4	4	4	BOUIE
	SI	7	7	7	

5		WHITE	YELLOW	RED	
	YDS	260	253	227	BUNKER
	PAR	4	4	4	HILL
	SI	15	15	13	

6		WHITE	YELLOW	RED	
	YDS	412	405	350	LOCH
	PAR	4	4	4	LOMOND
	SI	5	5	5	

7		WHITE	YELLOW	RED	
	YDS	408	397	242	SEAWARD
	PAR	4	4	4	
	SI	1	1	9	

8		WHITE	YELLOW	RED	
	YDS	371	359	352	SUNDOWNER
	PAR	4	4	4	
	SI	9	9	3	

9		WHITE	YELLOW	RED	
	YDS	131	126	108	OLD LUSS
	PAR	3	3	3	ROAD
	SI	17	17	17	

7 Seaward. 408 yards. Par 4. Stroke index 1.

Tiger: Take your line from Gourock Pier and then draw your drive with the object of finishing on the left of the fairway on the upslope to leave a mid-to-short iron directly at the flag.

Rabbit: (PS 7, W 5). South west winds make this drive over a long carry a frightening feat unless you boast single figures (why are they reading this?). The 6th fairway is nearer. The presence of six bunkers makes this over-sadistic.

8 Sundowner. 371 yards. Par 4. Stroke index 9.

Tiger: A good drive will fly the top of the hill and run on, leaving often no more than a wedge to the green. A 3 is always possible.

Rabbit: (PS 3, W 2). This should be a respite between the 7th and 9th, but at our level the transverse and left ditches loom large. I well remember the joy of reaching the fairway even though it was via the little bridge (not that long ago). The unexpected out of bounds behind the green has sickened many a medalist.

9 Old Luss Road. 131 yards. Par 3. Stroke index 17.

Tiger: A short iron, rarely more than a No.9, will suffice. Aim to finish below the hole for an attacking birdie putt.

Rabbit: (PS 1, W 10). This shot is probably a dawdle to visitors, but has wrecked many a card. The unique out of bounds on the Old Luss Road just short of the green, trees and rough seems to enter the psyche of many regulars. The most remarkable par resulted from a drive into the trees, a penalty drop on the 4th tee and a wedge into the hole.

Adding the score at this stage can seriously damage your prospects.

10 Clyde View. 447 yards. Par 4. Stroke index 2.

Tiger: Favour the right with your drive and the contours will bring your ball back to the middle of the fairway at the bottom of the hill for a medium-iron second. A real par 4.

Rabbit: (PS8, W2). A favourite vista though the fairway bunkers are fierce and a hook can enhance our knowledge of wildlife. Seeking my ball once I stepped on some unseen

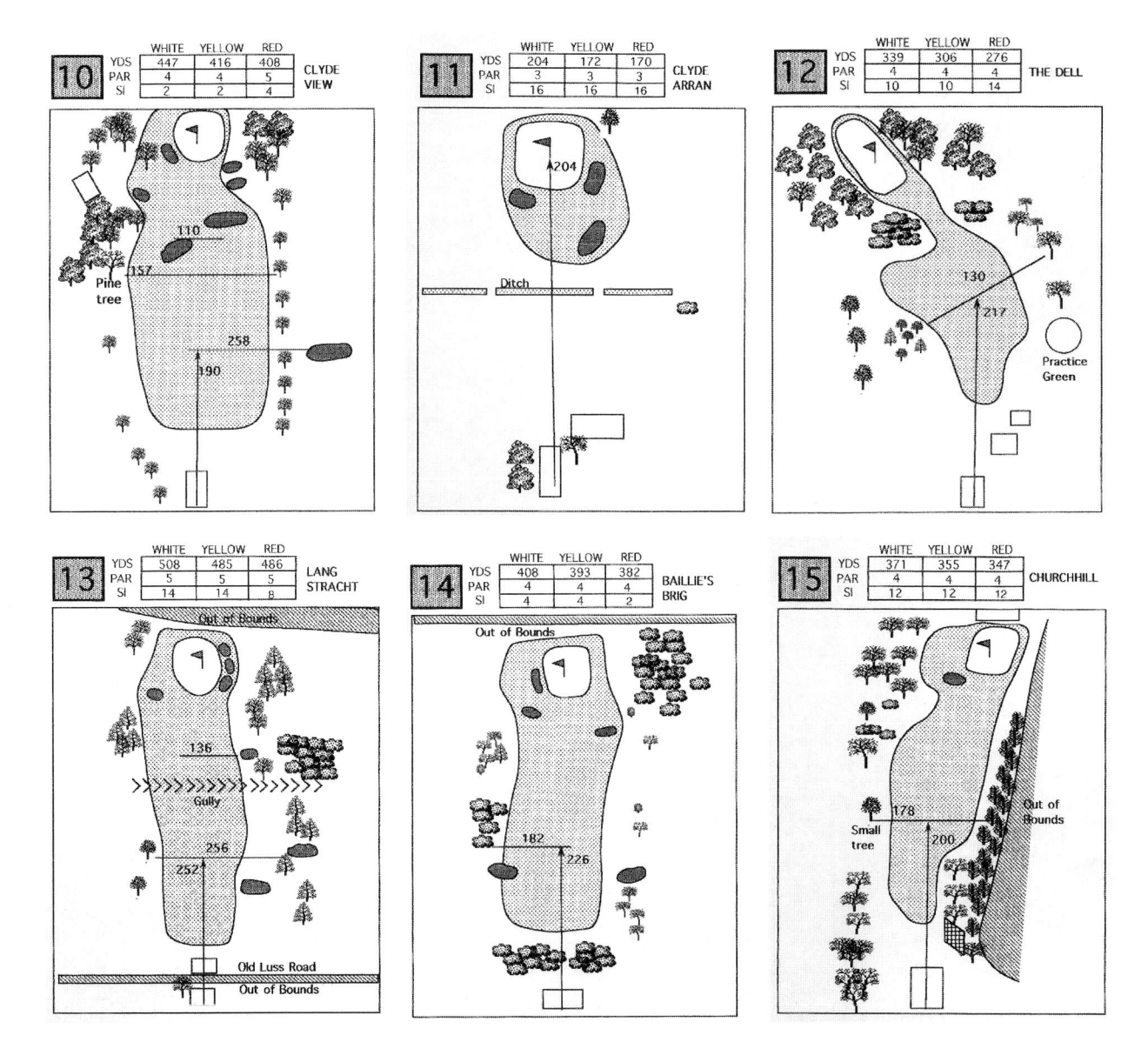

10	WHITE	YELLOW	RED	
YDS	447	416	408	CLYDE VIEW
PAR	4	4	5	
SI	2	2	4	

11	WHITE	YELLOW	RED	
YDS	204	172	170	CLYDE ARRAN
PAR	3	3	3	
SI	16	16	16	

12	WHITE	YELLOW	RED	
YDS	339	306	276	THE DELL
PAR	4	4	4	
SI	10	10	14	

13	WHITE	YELLOW	RED	
YDS	508	485	486	LANG STRACHT
PAR	5	5	5	
SI	14	14	8	

14	WHITE	YELLOW	RED	
YDS	408	393	382	BAILLIE'S BRIG
PAR	4	4	4	
SI	4	4	2	

15	WHITE	YELLOW	RED	
YDS	371	355	347	CHURCHHILL
PAR	4	4	4	
SI	12	12	12	

buttocks. I feared retribution but received only a breathless "Thank you". Who said this was a par 4?

11 **Clyde Arran. 204 yards. Par 3. Stroke index 16.**
Tiger: *In damp conditions fly the green, when dry take two clubs less and land your ball just across the front right bunker and the contours will do the rest. Don't expect a birdie.*

Rabbit: *(PS 7, W 8). A superb view (the hills of Arran can be seen on a clear day towering above the Kilpatricks) tempered by the longest par 3 on the course, heavily bunkered and open to gales. The bow of the Captayanis, the grounded sugar boat in the middle of the Clyde, gives a good line, but the rhoddy bush awaits. Recommended club may be the wedge or driver according to tee and weather.*

12 **The Dell. 339 yards. Par 4. Stroke index 10.**
Tiger: *Keep the driver in the bag and select a club which will leave you short of the gap and ideally to the right of it. From there it is just a little pitch, but check the pin position before choosing your club. There is approximately a two-club difference between the front and back of the green. A little care and you could have a birdie.*

Rabbit: *(PS 4, W 6). A most interesting hole for those who use an iron to the entrance. Others who find the old river bed can choose between a lost ball or a fearty tap forwards. Visitors should play 90 degrees north for the drive then 20 degrees north for the second.*

13 **Lang Stracht. 508 yards. Par 5. Stroke index 14**
Tiger: *A better eagle chance than the first. A long enough drive and you may be selecting a club for the second which, because of the bunker short and left and a left-to-right sloping green, should be played with a slight draw. In reality the hole is a par 4.*

Rabbit: *(PS 10, W 2). No help from the handicap here and there is a baby ravine to visit (better now than later when it has matured on the 14th and 17th). Dog-walkers hit from the medal tee would produce an interesting legal study.*

97 HELENSBURGH GOLF CLUB CENTENARY

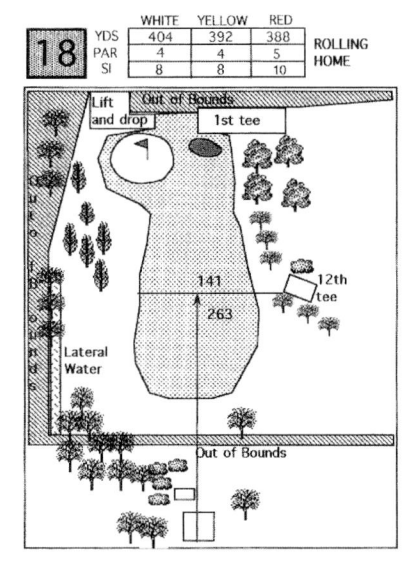

16	YDS	WHITE 150	YELLOW 148	RED 147	THE QUARRY
	PAR	3	3	3	
	SI	18	18	18	

17	YDS	WHITE 379	YELLOW 370	RED 368	DUE WEST
	PAR	4	4	4	
	SI	6	6	6	

18	YDS	WHITE 404	YELLOW 392	RED 388	ROLLING HOME
	PAR	4	4	5	
	SI	8	8	10	

14 **Baillie's Brig. 408 yards. Par 4. Stroke index 4.**

Tiger: A long draw will leave you over the brow of the hill and ideally on the left side of the fairway for a clear view of the pin. Fly the green to avoid unpredictable bounces. A difficult green to read and unless close to the pin the first putt should not be too aggressive.

Rabbit: (PS 6, W 7). The jungly ravine specialises in players who receive two shots at this hole. For those who make it over, thinking players will aim right with their second to allow for the slope - and find the bunker. The Old Luss Road awaits an overlong approach. (Quiz: On how many holes does the road affect play? Entries, written on a new golf ball, to the author please).

15 **Churchill. 371 yards. Par 4. Stroke index 12.**

Tiger: Favour the left with the drive and the slope will bring the ball back to the middle. The steep dip insists that the second is flown all the way to the green, but before selecting your club note whether the pin is on the upper or lower tier. This could mean the difference between a par and a birdie.

Rabbit: (PS 5, W 6). Bouncing a drive off the guard fence is not on - it may go straight through. A slicer's nightmare - my best result came from a ricochet from a fence spike into the hole. Look out for ball salesmen aged seven years on the right. They could be selling yours.

16 **The Quarry. 150 yards. Par 3. Stroke index 18.**

Tiger: A small patch of unseen fairway just beyond the first bunkers makes this hole one club longer than it looks. The green is the flattest on the course, making it the best birdie chance of the par 3s.

Rabbit: (PS 4, W 10). Deserving a chapter rather than a paragraph. The psychological effect has been known to cause lady members to devise their own tee on the other side. Enjoy your visit to the quarry - the shrubs and flowers are lovely and in the summer there are butterflies. Double pleasure is provided by nine bunkers left to play, each filled with concrete mix, caster sugar, self-raising flour and, for the hell of it, sand. Single-figure men should have a rebate for missing all this fun.

An 18-shot difference is needed to get relief.

17 **Due West. 379 yards. Par 4. Stroke index 6.**

Tiger: A straightforward drive, ideally to the left of the fairway, and a middle to short iron will set up a birdie putt.

Rabbit: (PS 6, W 8). See the 14th for ravine problems and add taller trees for the slicer. A hooked approach could end near the 15th tee - but at least we are facing the bar. Putts may be performed to a background of jeering from acquaintances leaving the 14th green, but revenge comes when they drive off the 15th.

A John Rees golfing adventure: Our hero demonstrates the "Rabbit" route at the 16th - tee shot into the quarry, second shot into even deeper trouble and still our man perseveres. His secret is not to get upset but to enjoy the wildlife, secure in the knowledge that this is a pleasure denied to low handicappers.
Pictures by Jim Stark.

18 Rolling Home. 404 yards. Par 4. Stroke index 8.

Tiger: A great finishing hole. The wide fairway invites you to open your shoulders, so go for it. The further up the fairway you are the easier it is to flight the second on to the green, a stage in front of the clubhouse. The putting surface is relatively flat inviting a closing birdie.

Rabbit: (PS 6, W 6). Old knees are wobbly by now, but a last effort will cross dog-watchers, golf lessons, road and hedge. A wide choice of shots is now available - out of bounds, stream, trees, putting area and clubhouse window. The stream could be re-opened to its full length - after I am gone.

Why do I love this course so much? Happy hacking to all."

The Rabbit Route may be the familiar one to most, but the Tiger Route has occasionally been taken, and we include here a blow-by-blow account of the best round ever played over the course as it exists today. It was a 64, five under par, and was compiled by Helensburgh member Alan Scott in the Breingan Medal on June 8, 1985.

The round was played in good weather over soft ground and to receptive greens. All pins were located near the back, some extremely far back, except the 16th where it was in the middle. There was a brief shower at the tenth where Scott registered his only bogey after donning his waterproofs while waiting to play his second shot.

Scott, who prepared for his momentous round by knocking back two gin and tonics beforehand and munching a Mars bar on his way up the first, credited his iron play for the success and even felt that his score

Alan Scott: superb iron play led to a course record 64.

could have been better. Had he not missed several short putts he might have broken 60. The details, with halves of 29 and 35, are:

1 (birdie 3): *Drive, pitch to just behind the pin, one putt.*
2 (par 4): *Drive, No.4 iron to back fringe, two putts from nine feet.*
3 (par 3): *No.5 iron to back right five yards off the green, pitch to five feet below the pin, one putt.*
4 (par 4): *Drive, wedge to back fringe, two putts from five feet.*
5 (par 4): *Drive and wedge to five feet, two putts.*
6 (birdie 3): *Drive and No.7 iron to eight feet, one putt.*
7 (birdie 3): *Drive and No.5 iron to five feet behind the pin, one putt.*
8 (birdie 3): *Drive to the top of the hill, pulled No.7 iron, holed pitch.*
9 (birdie 2): *No.9 iron to back fringe, holed downhill putt from five feet.*
10 (bogey 5): *Drive, No.4 iron short, chip to three feet, two putts.*
11 (par 3): *No.3 iron, two putts.*
12 (par 4): *Drive, No.9 iron to eight feet, two putts.*
13 (birdie 4): *Drive, No.4 wood just short, chip to four feet, one putt.*
14 (par 4): *Drive, No.6 iron to 12 feet, two putts.*
15 (par 4): *Drive, No.9 iron to six feet, two putts.*
16 (par 3): *No.8 iron to 20 feet, first putt six feet past, holed return.*
17 (par 4): *Drive, No.7 iron to six feet, two putts.*
18 (par 4): *Drive, No.6 iron to 18 feet, two putts.*

This record, at the time of writing, has stood for seven years, is better than any performance even by a professional, and may well last until the course is next altered. There again, Scott himself feels it could have been as many as five strokes better, and those sentiments suggest it is very much there to be beaten. The next time you tee off it could be your day . . .

There is no existence of a ladies record which means it is up for grabs in centenary year.

Epilogue

Some thoughts of Confusedius

Helensburgh Golf Club, an August 2020 vision.

It seems but only yesterday when the club had its centenary, but 27 years have passed. Some changes have taken place but many things remain the same. Sitting here in front of the roaring fire in the library of the new clubhouse, sheltered from the howling wind and pouring rain of an August Saturday afternoon, the silence broken only by the chink of glasses, click of snooker balls, Tom Reid's laugh and Jim Barrowman's snores, reminiscences came flooding to mind.

It is hard to believe that the "Wimpey Gardens" was once part of the golf course and to remember the old changing shack. The new clubhouse majestically straddling the peat bogs is a tribute to the members who designed it. Sandy Houston's dark green corrugated roof blends in with the surroundings and complements Jim Barrowman's Lilley blue breeze blocks.

Joe Craig was the inspiration behind the successful nearby ladies' clubhouse into which it is proposed to install central heating, or for that matter any form of heating or lighting, in the near future. The equalisation of women's membership conditions and the necessary increase in their fees is a thing of the past, although there was a little resentment that no more weekend tee times could be allocated due to the demand from members (ordinary, male).

The luxury and facilities of the men's clubhouse are very much admired. The linoleum in the changing rooms is a big improvement and the Jim Brown amusement arcade is very popular. With the benefit of hindsight Jimmy Ramsay's suggestion that we get two Jacuzzi so that they could breed was inappropriate.

The addition of a filthy bar to complement the dirty and gay bars was a great success and the introduction of rails to control queues at the bar has stopped Jimmy Cavana pushing in. Jim Stark's courtesy bus service is very popular although inviting the traffic police in for a gin proved imprudent.

The 27 hole course has settled down well and the novelty of grass on the fairways has worn off. The par 11 Ben Bouie hole is the main feature of the layout and the donation of a chairlift by Frank Platt has made it an easier hole.

John Ashworth originally complained about the six hour rounds until it was agreed finally that it was not necessary to go round the full 27 holes. The arrangement with Tom Reid for clearing the fairways of snow has extended the playing season.

The membership remains very strong, but because Alan Christianson's geriatric group has now grown to 216 members the waiting list for juvenile membership extends to 29 years. The appointment of Douglas Dalgleish as junior vice president to George Leaf in preparation for Douglas's retirement was well received in that he no longer feels a need to cause arguments.

The Brunton Miller Flywheel and Shyster Winter League remains very popular and now extends to 32 weeks. With an entry of 380, sales of sweaters have soared.

We have been very lucky with the captains we have had over the period. Jim Barrowman was very popular during his period with his policy of free White Shields for all, but this was tempered when he abolished the committee system and assumed the role of dictator. Compulsory wearing of dinner jackets in the gay bar was not well received.

Willie Gracie was always available for consultation in the bar and this service was rewarded by his appointment as course manager, as successor to Ronnie Myles who was seconded to Loch Lomond Golf Club for their staging of the Ryder Cup. Gracie's move capitalised on his training as the Barrowman gardener, although it has been noted that the hedges on the course are extremely unkempt.

Robert Cunningham-Graham's period as captain ended sadly. When the Friday evening group was trapped by the blizzard of '99 and stranded in the clubhouse for two weeks and liquid refreshments ran very low in spite of Sandy Barclay's helicopter deliveries, Robert made the final sacrifice and walked out in the blizzard to give the others a better chance of survival. He is much missed.

Some of the members have prospered over the years. Gordon Hattle recently sold out to Ratners who were looking for a complementary product range. His closing down 'rummage' day, whereby you could search for your own watch or at least a similar one, was well supported and 'the little old lady from Cardross with a white dog' was finally reunited with her timepiece. Gone now are the days of craftsmanship and service.

Relationships with the media improved significantly

when Douglas Lowe took over as editor of the Advertiser and gave over space previously covering minority sports such as football to coverage of the golf club. His introduction of a women's feature in the paper was warmly welcomed, particularly when telephone numbers were included. It was a tribute to Douglas when the Helensburgh centenary book outsold The History of the Universe.

Colin Dalgleish continues to bring credit to the club through his 27 years as Scottish captain. It was a bold move to select David Yorke and Fraser McCathie for the national team and one which really ought to have brought further credit to the club, although what happened did not surprise Alec Dunlop.

Tom Inglis made a bold move when he took over the ailing Ford Motor Corporation which is now a subsidiary of Strathford. Regrettably this means that Tom does not get many 'freebies' any more and since he became captain of the Ayr over-60s rugby team, members see a limited amount of him.

Donald McDonald completed Faslane eventually and moved on to try to finish Spain. Fortunately, with his nine months holiday a year we continue to see a lot of him. During his successful year of captaincy he broke all records for the number of hands shaken.

When Robert Prow got the contract for panel beating Trident his business boomed, although there were unfair

Gordon Hattle presents Evan McGregor with an item of silverware during Festival of Golf Week. It was ostensibly the Midway Trophy - but can we be sure it was not just any old cup?
Picture: Helensburgh Advertiser.

suggestions that this coincided with the appointment of Frank Shields as relief Trident driver.

After years of paying daily instalments, Jimmy Nicholson owns the taxi company, and his 50% discount for club members has now made him popular.

When John Ashworth joined the committee as house convener, Douglas Dalgleish's aspirations of winning the J & B Order of Merit were finally dashed by the Chivas Regal takeover of the bar stocks.

Robert Burns has now developed a technique for repairing television sets and members were delighted that his successful shoulder replacement operations made this possible.

Regrettably there have been some disappointments over the years although when Gordon Hattle snapped the Centenary Putter it was probably more of a frustrated rather than a malicious act.

Harry Fazal should shortly be released from custody following his court marshal. He probably would have got away with dropping Trident, but when he sent up a missile on Guy Fawkes night problems followed.

When Evan McGregor's hair turned black the worst was feared until John Harper diagnosed that the dark rum table had risen which meant that the hair roots were now in it.

CRAFT, an association concerned with failing memory (it stands for Can't Remember A Thing - including what F stands for), was founded by Gordon Hattle in 1992 or thereabouts and now has an enormous membership although the attendance at meetings is small because few can remember where and when they take place.

The UK membership of the European Community did not last long and our fees are now 27,000,000 yen.

Bertie Weir returned safely from his trip to Buckingham Palace by 2000cc, 48 valve motor cycle with which his police escort failed to keep up. He decided to save the Royal Family from the expense of a telegram.

Jim Stark has just joined me, a pint in one hand and a G&T in the other, looking for these few notes to incorporate in the bicentenary book he is writing.

J.A.

AUTHORS' NOTE

We have resisted titling the book "A History of Helensburgh Golf Club" because of a worry that the story is incomplete as a result of the absence of most of the minutes books and a general dearth of archival material. We have made our best attempt but would not like the result to be considered an end in itself. The intention henceforth is to keep the archives continually up to date and through this process omissions and errors which may be spotted by readers can be logged for future reference.